PASSION FRUIT

PANDORA PRESS FICTION

PASSION FRUIT

Romantic fiction with a twist

Edited by Jeanette Winterson

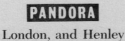
London, and Henley

This collection first published in 1986
by Pandora Press (Routledge & Kegan Paul plc)

14 Leicester Square, London WC2H 7PH, England and

Broadway House, Newtown Road,
Henley on Thames, Oxon RG9 1EN, England

Set in Sabon
by Columns of Reading
and printed in Great Britain
by The Guernsey Press Co. Ltd.
Guernsey, Channel Islands.

British Library Cataloguing in Publication Data
Passion fruit: romantic fiction with a twist.
1. Love stories, English
I. Winterson, Jeanette
823'.085'08[FS]   PR1309.L6

ISBN 0-86358-070-X

CONTENTS

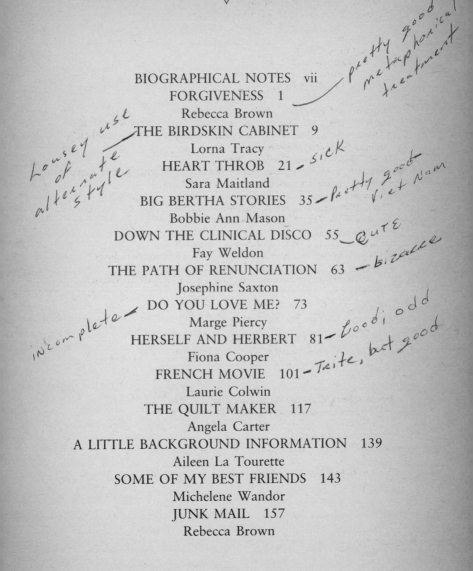

BIOGRAPHICAL NOTES

♡

Rebecca Brown lives in Seattle. Her work has appeared in a number of magazines and short story collections, including *Mae West is Dead* (ed. Adam Mars-Jones, Faber, 1983). Her first collection of stories, *Evolution of Darkness*, was published by Brilliance Books in 1984, and her first novel, *The Haunted House*, will be published by Picador and Viking in 1986. She has no children.

Lorna Tracy is an American, long resident in Newcastle upon Tyne, where she lives with her husband, Jon Silkin. For the past sixteen years she has been a co-editor of the literary quarterly *Stand*. In 1981 Virago published a collection of her short stories, *Amateur Passions*, and she is currently completing her first novel, also for Virago. Her stories have appeared in a number of journals, including the *London Review of Books*, and she writes regularly for *Words*.

Sara Maitland married an Anglican curate in 1972 and has two children. Her first novel won the 1978 Somerset Maugham Award, her second, *Virgin Territory*, was published by Michael Joseph in 1984. She has written two volumes of short stories – *Telling Tales* (Journeyman), and *Weddings and Funerals* with Aileen La Tourette

(Brillance Books) — and is at present working on a biography of Vesta Tilly for Virago.

Bobbie Ann Mason was born in 1940 and lives in Pennsylvania. Her first book, *Shiloh and Other Stories*, won the Pan-Hemingway award. Her second, *In Country*, was published by Harper & Row and Chatto in autumn 1985.

Fay Weldon is the author of seven novels and two volumes of short stories, the most recent of which was *Polaris and Other Stories* (Hodder, 1985).

Josephine Saxton lives in Warwickshire, England, and is training to be an acupuncturist. Her work has appeared in countless magazines, and a collection of her Science Fiction stories, *The Power of Time*, was published by Chatto in 1985. Pandora plan to publish a second collection, *Little Tours of Hell*, in 1986.

Marge Piercy lives in Massachusetts with Ira Wood. She is the author of nine books of poetry, including *Stone, Paper, Knife* (Pandora Press, 1983) and seven novels.

Fiona Cooper is a new young writer living in London. Her first novel, *Life and Times of Rotary Spokes*, is likely to be published by Brilliance Books in 1986.

Laurie Colwin lives in New York and is the author of three novels (*Shine on, Bright and Dangerous Object*; *Happy All the Time*; *Family Happiness*) and two collections of short stories.

Angela Carter was born in 1940. She is the author of numerous novels, short stories and essays, including her most recent success, *Nights at the Circus* (Chatto, 1984). A film has been made of one of her short stories, 'The Company of Wolves'.

Aileen La Tourette was brought up in New Jersey and now lives in England with her two sons. She has written a number of radio plays and short stories, including *Weddings and Funerals* with Sara Maitland (Brilliance Books, 1984). Her first novel, *Nuns and Mothers*, was published by Virago in 1984; her second, *Cry Wolf*, will be published by them in 1986.

Michelene Wandor is a poet, playwright and critic. Recent work includes a feature about Jean Rhys for Radio 4 and an eight-part dramatisation of *The Brothers Karamazov* by Dostoyevsky. A collection of her short stories, many on Jewish themes, particularly that of the Dybbuk, *Guests in the Body*, will be published by Virago in early 1986.

Jeanette Winterson was born in Lancashire in 1959. Her first novel, *Oranges are not the Only Fruit*, was published by Pandora in 1985. Her second, *Boating for Beginners*, was published by Methuen, also in 1985. Her unusual fitness book, *Fit for the Future*, will be published by Pandora in 1986. She has just completed a third novel and wonders what to do next . . .

FORGIVENESS

♡

Rebecca Brown

When I said I'd give my right arm for you, I didn't think you'd ask me for it, but you did.

You said, 'Give it to me.'

And I said, 'OK.'

There were lots of reasons I gave it to you.

First of all, I didn't want to be made a liar of. (I have never lied to you.) So when you reminded me that I'd said it and asked me if I really meant it, I didn't want to seem like I was copping out by saying that I'd only spoken figuratively. (It is an old saying, after all.) Also, I had the feeling you didn't think I would really do it, that you were testing me to see if I would, and I wanted you to know I would.

Also, I believed you wouldn't have asked me for it unless you realy wanted it, and needed it.

But then, when you got it, you bronzed it and put it on the mantel over the fireplace in the den.

The night you took it, I dreamt of arms. I slept on the couch in the den because I was still bleeding, even through the bandages, and I knew I'd stir during the night and need to put on more bandages and we didn't want me to wake you up. So I stayed on the couch, and when I slept, I dreamt of arms: red arms, blue arms, golden arms. And arms made out of jade. Arms with tattoos, arms with stripes. Arms waving,

1

sleeping, holding. Arms that rested up against my ribs.

We kept my arm in the bathtub, bleeding like a fish. When I went to bed, the water was color of rose water, with thick red lines like strings. And when I woke up the first time to change my bandages, it was colored like salmon. Then it was carnation red, and then maroon, then burgundy, then purple, thick, and almost black by morning.

In the morning, you took it out. I watched you pat it dry with my favorite big fat terry cloth towel and wrap it in Saranwrap and take it out and get it bronzed.

I learned to do things differently. To button up my shirts, to screw and unscrew tight the toothpaste cap, to tie my shoes. We didn't think of this. Together, we were valiant, brave and stoic. Though I couldn't quite keep up with you at tennis anymore.

In a way, it was fun. Things I once took for granted became significant. Cutting a steak with a knife and fork, or buttoning my fly, tying a string around a package, adding milk while stirring.

After a while, I developed a scab and you let me come back to bed. But sometimes in the night, I'd shift or have a nightmare, jolt, and suddenly, I'd open up again, and bleed all over, uncontrollably. The first time this happened neither of us could go back to sleep. But after a while, you got used to it and you'd be back asleep in a minute. It didn't seem to bother you at all.

But I guess after a while it started bothering you, because one day when I was washing out the sheets I'd bloodied the night before, you said, 'You sleep too restless. I don't like it when your bleeding wakes me up. I think you're sick. I think it's sick to cut off your own arm.'

I looked at you, your sweet brown eyes, innocent as a

puppy. 'But you cut it off,' I said. 'You did it.' You didn't blink. 'You asked me for it, so I said OK.'

'Don't try to make me feel guilty,' you said, your pretty brown eyes looking straight at me. 'It was your arm.'

You didn't blink.

I closed my eyes.

That night I bled again. I woke up and the bed was red, all full of blood and wet. I reached over to touch you and to wake you up and tell you I was sorry, but you were not there.

I learned more. To cook and clean, to eat a quarter-pounder with one fist, to balance my groceries on my knee while my hand fumbled with the front door key.

My arm got strong. My left sleeve on my shirts got tight and pinched. My right shirt sleeve was lithe and open, carefree, like a pretty girl.

But then the novelty wore off. I had to convince myself. I read about those valiant cases, one-legged heroes who run across the continent to raise money for causes, and paraplegic mothers of four, one-eyed pool sharks. I hoped these stories would inspire me, but they didn't. I didn't want to be like those people. I didn't want to be cheery and valiant. I didn't want to rise above my situation. What I wanted was my arm.

Because I missed it. I missed everything about it. I missed the long solid weight of it in my sleeve. I missed clapping and waving and putting my hand in my pocket. I missed waking up at night with it twisted behind my head, asleep and heavy and tingling.

And then I realized that I had missed these things all along, the whole time my arm had been over the mantel, but that I'd never said anything or even let myself feel anything bad because I didn't want to dwell on those feelings because I didn't want to make you feel bad and I didn't want you to think I wanted you to feel bad.

I decided to look for it. Maybe you'd sold it. You were always good with things like that.

I hit the pawnshops. I walked into them and they'd ask me could they help me and I'd say, 'I'm looking for an arm.' And they'd stare at me, my empty sleeve pinned empty to my shirt, or flapping in the air.

After I'd searched all the local pawnshops, I started going to ones further away. I saw a lot of the country. It was nice. And I got good at it. The more I did, the more I learned to do. The braver ones would look at me directly in the eye. They'd give me the names and addresses of outlets selling artificial limbs, or reconstructive surgeons. But I didn't want another one, I wanted mine. And then, the more I looked for it, the more I wondered if I wasn't looking more for something else besides my severed arm. I wondered, was I really searching for you?

It all came clear to me. Like something ripped from me. You'd done this to me as a test. To show me things. To show me what things meant to me, how much my arm was part of me, but how I could learn to live without it. How, if I was forced to, I could learn how to get by with only part of me, with next to nothing. You'd done this to me to teach me something.

And then I thought how, if you were testing me, you must be watching me, to see if I was passing.

So, I started acting out my life for you, because I felt you watching all my actions. I whistled with bravado, jaunted, rather than walked, with a confident swagger. I slapped friendly pawnshop keepers on their shoulders and told them jokes. I was fun, an inspiration they'd remember after I'd passed through.

I acted like I couldn't care less about my old arm. I

4

liked the peaceful breezes in my sleeve.

I began to think in perfect sentences, as if you were listening to me. I thought clear sentences inside myself. I said, 'I get along just fine without my arm.' I think that I convinced myself, in trying to convince you, that I had never had an arm I'd lost.

Soon I didn't think the word inside me any more. I didn't think about the right hand gloves all buried in the bottom of my drawer.

I made myself not miss it. I tested myself. I sat in the den and stared at the empty space above the mantel. I spent the night on the couch. I went into the bathroom and looked in the tub. I felt nothing. I went to bed.

I thought my trips to pawnshops, my wanderlust, were only things I did to pass the time. I thought of nothing almost happily.

I looked at my shoulder. The tissue was sweet and smooth. I ran my fingers over it. Round and slightly puffed, pink and shiny and slick. As soft as pimento, as cool as a spoon, the tenderest flesh of my body.

My beautiful empty sleeve and I were friends, like intimates.

So everything was fine.
For a while.
Then you came back.
Then everything did.

But I was careful. It had been a long time. I had learned how to live. Why, hadn't I just forgotten what used to fill my empty sleeve entirely? I was very careful. I acted like nothing had ever been different, that you had never ripped it out of me, then bronzed it, put it on the mantel, left with it. I wanted things to stay forgot.

And besides, it was so easy, so familiar having you around. It was nice.

I determined to hold on to what I'd learned. About the strength of having only one.

Maybe I should have told you then. But, I told myself, if you knew to leave it alone, then good. And if you didn't know, we needed to find that out.

So we were sitting in the den. You looked at me with your big sweet pretty brown eyes and you said, you whispered it softly like a little girl, you said, 'Oh, I'm so sorry.' You started crying softly, your lips quivering. 'Can you ever forgive me all of this?' You said it slow and sweet like a foreign language. I watched you, knowing you knew the way I was watching you. You leaned into me and pulled my arm around you and ran your pretty fingers down the solid muscle in my sleeve. 'Just hold me, darling,' you said. 'Just hold me again.'

I ran my wet palm, shaking, on your gorgeous back. Your hair smelled sweet.

I looked at your beautiful tear-lined face and tried to pretend that I had never seen you before in my life.

'Why did you do it?' I whispered.

You looked at me, your eyes all moist and sweet like you could melt anything in the world. You didn't answer.

'What did you do with it?'

You shrugged your shoulders, shook your head and smiled at me sweeter than an angel.

'Say something,' I whispered into your pretty hair. 'Say something, goddammit.'

You looked up at me and your sweet angel eyes welled up with tears again. You put your head against my breast and sobbed.

You made me rock you and I did and then you cried yourself to sleep as innocent as a baby. When you were asleep I walked you to the bedroom and put you to bed. You slept. I watched you all night. You remembered nothing in the morning.

In the morning we had coffee. You chatted to me about your adventures. You cocked your head at just the right places, the way I remembered you did. You told me that you'd worked hard in the time you'd been away. You told me you had grown. You told me how much you had learned about the world, about yourself, about honor, faith and trust, etc., etc. You looked deep into my eyes and said, 'I've changed.' You said how good and strong and true and truly different you were. How you had learned that it is not our acts, but our intents, that make us who we are.

I watched your perfect teeth.

I felt your sweet familiar hands run up my body, over the empty sleeve that rumpled on the exposed side of me. I closed my eyes and couldn't open them. My mouth was closed. I couldn't tell you anything.

I couldn't tell you that you can't re-do a thing that's been undone. I couldn't tell you anything that you would understand. I couldn't tell you that it wasn't just the fact that you had ripped it out of me and taken it and mounted it then left with it then lost it, how it wasn't only that, but it was more, how it was that when you asked me, I believed you and I told you yes, how, though I had tried a long time to replace what you had hacked away from me, I never could undo the action of your doing so, that I had, and only ever would have, more belief in your faulty memory, your stupid sloppy foresight, than in your claims of change. How I believed, yes, I believed with all my heart, that given time, you'd do something else again, some new and novel variant to what you'd done to me, again. And then I thought, but this was only half a thought, that even if you had changed, no, *really* changed, truly and at last, and even if you knew yourself better than I thought you did, and even if you knew me better than I know myself, and even if I'm better off than I've ever been, and even if this was the only way we could have gotten to this special place where we are now, and even if there's a reason, darling, something bigger than both of us, and even if all these 'even ifs' are true, that I would never believe you again, never forget what I know of you, never forget what you've done to me, what you will do, I'll never believe the myth of forgiveness between us.

THE BIRDSKIN CABINET

───────────── ♡ ─────────────

Lorna Tracy

Polyphemous sends a valentine to Galatea: *I've got my eye on you!* He is so pleased with this composition that he submits three hectograph copies of it to The Martian School of Poetry, where he hopes to enroll as a student. If he works really hard maybe he can even become an 'agency creative' at Snaatchi & Snaatchi. That would impress the beautiful Galatea, wouldn't it? American girls expect a lot, he knows that already.

On his way to the post office with Galatea's valentine in his bosom and the three hectograph copies stuck into the top of his britches Polyphemous gets another idea. He remembers that Galatea lives with her aunt. It would do his cause no harm if he saluted the aunt as well. So Polyphemous sits down on a convenient hill and adds a few words in his execrable handwriting, for he has left his typewriter at home: *PS. Greetings to your magnificent aunt.*

The morning of February 14th Galatea opens the valentine from Polyphemous.

> I've got my eye on you!
> Hottest regards from Guess Who?

Galatea groans at her admirer's ponderous couplet. Then, with difficulty, she decodes the handwritten postscript:

P.S. Greetings to your magnificent cunt.

When Galatea's boyfriend, Bernie Mainspring, a third year student in revenue enhancement at The Martian School of Monetarism, hears about the valentine from Polyphemous he urges Galatea to take the bullshit by the horns. Galatea says she's already taken it by the bushel basket.

(Bernie doesn't get it; it's a joke.)

'Bernie, who do you think I am – Europa? You know, really, Bernie, that Polyphemous is completely beyond the pale.'

'What pail are you talking about, beloved?' Bernie wonders.

'The Old Oaken Bucket, darling.'

'?'

'Oh, forget it, forget it.' Galatea reminds herself that all Bernie represents to her is an investment, the kind of mate that can see a girl through to the end of this wicked century. Galatea herself has no patience with the bears and bulls of commerce. She has other bucolic plans and someone like Bernie, who's into pork-bellies and destined for the Chicago Stock Exchange, complements them in the most conventional way.

Galatea's aunt thinks Bernie is Such a Suitable Young Man for her lovely niece. He reminds her of the nice young men she had known back at the other end of the century, the ones who either went to France and got slaughtered or else waited until 1929 and got slaughtered at home on Wall Street.

But alas, poor Galatea! Polyphemous is her fate. She hardly has a year teaching high school biology before the creationists seize control of the school system and she finds herself washed up on the northeast coast of a fierce and barbarous island.

ENGLAND AFTER THE DISILLUSION OF THE BRITISH VAMPIRE
or
GOD IS AN ENGLISHMAN
or
MARRIAGE
or
THE HERO'S REWARD
or
THE MAD WYF
or
THE STRUGGLE WITH THE VILLAIN DOES NOT ALWAYS END
IN VICTORY

It's like waiting for God's love, waiting for him. Elusive. Does it exist? Does he notice? Does he *care*? You are here in his house. He is here in his house as well. Listen: scruffy buskins stomping up and down the bare stone stairs. Up and down. Up and down. UP

AND

DOWN

Banging doors. Switching off lights. Our house, *our* house, he shouts.

Isolated in the middle of the bare yard the bird-table balances on a tall pole to thwart cats.

All spaced out up there along the gutter, the pigeons keep one eye on you, then the other. Something is going on here. Do you think they will seek vengeance?

They're certainly waiting for you. They crook their necks, cock the one eye, then the other. They hear you in the scullery running water, rattling pans. Tense and concentrated . . . feeling their fleas . . . racers on the blocks . . . ready . . . set . . .

11

STOP!

Stop those bloody pigeons from eating up the lot, he shouts.

Sometimes you bear the bird-table religiously on its pole, a solemn procession around the temple yard. (*I sat down under his shadow* . . .) On sunny days it's at least a shade over your head. But mostly, processions occur at night (. . . *and his banner over me was love.*)

The hawks and the eagles are more faithful than the birds of Paradise.

Herring gulls, rooks and blue-footed boobies consume the British vampire's dissolving substance. Something is going on here. Do you think they will seek vengeance?

He twists his neck in its oily rainbow ruff. His beak's bigger than his brain-pan.

Kitchens here are primitive; the sootfall – the devil's snowflakes – heavy and continual. Mixed with sea-fret and the shit of fish-eating birds it is Albion's atmosphere. It cannot be heated. Think of the millions of horses, cows, sheep grazing on the land. Animal flatulence pumps tons of methane into the air. You should feel warmer – yet you tremble, like the stars in January.

You know that the rhinencephalon is the oldest part of the cerebral hemispheres of the forebrain; the primitive, reptilian nose-brain; the Id. That the structures of the embryo cerebral cortex in a swift, imperial expansion soon overgrow the ancient brain, seal and conceal it, Ego and Superego. Now it seems to you that this ancient feature of the mammal brain, assumed to be but feebly developed within the skull of man, resembles the gross body of a termite queen, immobilized deep in the nest, controlling more than you dream, the aboriginal olfactory life of your kind; that the assumption of its atrophy and enfeeblement, of its perfectly natural supersession, only disguises the ramping suppression of a senior order; is treacherous Athena's perfidious work. By owl-light she has ranted you from your recanted altar, from the table spread with blood.

You fly to America with Polyphemous for a visit with your aunt. A strange woman introduces you to Bernie Mainspring. 'Meet my husband, Caveman,' she says. Bernie cringes imperceptibly, then comes right back with a big smile and reaches up and shakes hands with Polyphemous. Bernie's not quite as tall as the Doberman but he looks much nicer-natured. These days.

You give Bernie a big smile and tell him it's lovely to meet him (again), and Polyphemous puts his hands back into his pockets and an awkward silence is closing in when your aunt arrives with news that Monte and Zack next door have split. Monte got custody of the rabbit. Aunt seems happy with this.

Sometimes you imagine your brain as a castellated museum of natural history (ontogeny recapitulates phylogeny) with all its separate halls, its dead exhibits, for you eked out your college scholarship assisting in the birdskin cabinet, close to things that once had life and have it no longer.

'The farther you go, the closer you get,' says Aunt.

'To what?'

'To the end.'

JETEZ LE DANS LE CABINET! JETEZ LE DANS LE CABINET! shrieks her parrot, the only words it has.

The trouble is, you're a mated pair, you really are. He always comes back from the girlfriends. Sooner or later. He accuses you of making yourself look attractive so as 'to lure men whom then you brutally reject'. He insists that you're deeply flirtatious. Guess what he calls 'flirtatious'? Undressing at night in the bedroom and putting on a nightgown to sleep in. To sleep in. To get between the sheets in. To sleep. To rest. To doze. To drowse. To nap. To nod. To slumber. To achieve insensibility. To lie down in bed for purposes of repose. To seek the arms of Morpheus. To quaff of Lethe. To knit up the ravell'd sleave . . . Where else if not in your own bed?

Our bed, *our* bed, he shouts.

He lies there already, watching; lies in bed not wearing anything; lies there on his back, his erection poking up the sheet like a Big Top. 'You don't have to watch,' you tell him. You turn your back, as modest as a damsel. (As modest as a damsel used to be.)

'I suppose you could shoot him for food,' Aunt says.

He says that you are maladjusted and sends you to Scotland for analysis. Even on the train you go on working. You have papers to mark for The Open University. Exams. Piece-work.

WHAT THE PROFESSIONALS SAY

If our automobile breaks down we do not kick it, pray over it, or assume that its spirit has departed. We call the RAC. We apply rationality in problem solving. Why then doesn't the application of rationality to personality disorders result in altered behaviour?

'I forget,' you answer.

'Been lotus-eating, have you?'

'I still remember my own country.'

'Then remember why rationality fails to apply in cases like your own. Please try.'

'What is the text,' you ask.

'Sources of Gain in Psychotherapy.'

What is the burden, you demand.

— No correlation exists between insight and change in behaviour.

The eye leaps to any illusion of sunlight: yellow paint on a stone house, a tree turning in the autumn, a flowering of gorse so brilliant it seems to shine on the hills after dark like a city. But the practical gulls perch on small flues in Scotland to warm their arses in December. And you submit to an error in perception and sadly agree that the Scotch terrier you saw flying at a low altitude over the A69 was only a crow after all.

– Contemporary neuroses are frequently characterized not so much by repression and conversion as by an awful awareness and a merciless raw anxiety.

It's the dark of the year; the annual hour of 3 a.m. You know that the red shift says 'going away, going away'; that light guarantees itself no continuing source; that there are black holes in space where gravity, usually the weakest of natural forces, is unquestionably the strongest, able to trap and dismantle the light.

Siege clouds surround the cold centuries; thunderous shadows bruise the sea. The earth stones you. You are hurt by the ground, bearing its brochs and stone cradles indifferently, so that they fall into pieces, the stones separating from one another.

In the past this has led to a great deal of misunderstanding and poetry.

– The problem of the contemporary neurotic is not lack of insight but lack of identity, of purpose, of meaning in life.

Owner and sole proprietor of the Pandora Box Company Ltd., mild as gravity, shipping dreamwork between England and Edinburgh twice a week by courier in bone bonnet up and down these tracks all year – you **are** the skull and crossbones. The value of your freight, its dangerous properties, not evident. No implication of briefcase or strapped tin canister, and what you carry in your canvas bag are other people's griefs, on them to ride in judgement. It is your job to; it is of some social value.

– Nothing can make a person more anxious or more guilty than an unrelentingly clear appreciation of the absurd and desperate condition of man today.

You choose a carriage where smoking, if discovered, is fined for – in fact, twenty-five quid. You smoke, but don't here. By your own choice, prohibited. You imagine you have seen smoking for what it is: mere visible proof of a capacity for respiration and today you have nothing to prove.

Immature female voices surround you, and middle-aged female bodies. They are Amerc'n Tursts in Yerp; WASP widows abroad on a post-bereavement tour, their husbands deep-sixed forever. Each of them had lived many years of wedlock in a space that an arm could reach across but didn't. Was that not harder than death's fixed gulf?

You listen to their dialogue and consider a dialogue of your own, the presumptuousness of the notion diminishing, as reverence does, with familiarity. One might add something, with respect, to creation. How would it go?

– Look! The snowy Cheviots!

– No, only a bank of healthier clouds rising in the west.

– Can they deliver themselves, any more than those above us now with shut bellies decaying? Stillborn Christmas snow.

– Another barren year?

– I don't love you.

– Don't we do loving things for one another?

– But I don't love you.

– Marriage? A child?

– I don't mind. But I'm content just to go on living as

we do.

A continuum; you can get on anywhere. As good played backwards as forwards. The passionate indifference. The skyful of rotting clouds, grey with the mouldy snow that can't be shed.

In your child's dream you were a pallid circle, like his father, also a pale, brown circle. Where the two circles met, began in a sliding encroachment to lie, one over the other, your child in his dream began. The ellipse thus bitten out of both circles was his own red life. The colour not drawn from you. His own colour, not made from anything else. Nothing mixed your child, encroaching your two full circles, making each one less, taking substance from them. There in his dream was your child; his immaculate blood.

Holy Island. From the railway Lindisfarne Castle on its rock resembles a sinking liner going down, bows up, into the sea. Soon now the flesh-pink strand at Berwick upon Tweed where the long veins of water swell and burst, foam gushing out along the lateral rip you can see opening the length of the wave. The sea throws itself upon the sands like a drowning man and slips back. No purchase. No rest. Out at sea three whale-shaped cumuli are arranged across the overcast in proportionately diminishing sizes like an advertisement for clouds in three price ranges.

'You can't **buy** a washrag in this country,' says one of the widows, whose hair is the colour and texture of the lint that gathers under beds from time to time, all body ash and animal danders. She wears the nacreous tumours of oysters in the lobes of her ears. Why should the codling not wear this widow's sarcoma as a flourish in his buttonhole? Why should the widow say but the codling, ha-ha, has no coat? He has his hole, dear lady. He has his anal vent.

'Say, look at that boat!' another widow cries.

Tell her about it. Reveal your own American voice to them now. They would gather you up with joy.

It is a small Dutch cargo vessel that has been athwart the channel for ten days now, glowering, bows on, at Tweedmouth. What holds a stuck ship upright after the tide has gone out from under it in this case, ladies, is six hundred tons of rock in the hold. Now you begin to feel almost local by comparison, being only sixty miles from the city where you live in a country that is not your own.

The widows want postcards. They ask each other, what is this place?

'This is Burr-wick upon Tweed,' says one. They wonder, how can she tell?

'I can see a sign,' she answers.

You could also tell them that some centuries ago two young women here showed Aeneas Silvius 'to a chamber strewn with straw, planning to sleep with him, as was the custom of the country, if they were asked.' But Aeneas Silvius ignored them, 'thinking less about women than about robbers, and he took the fact that no robber came in the night as a reward for his continence.' You could add one fact concerning his subsequent life, for some time after he left Berwick upon Tweed he became Pope Pius II. Finally, you could describe to them how this small city seen from the station's heights at night, spread out on either side of the estuary where the river grows thin at low tide, seems to billow under its zircon lights as though the wind had worked beneath the ground and puffed it up. How the beacon on the Farne Islands blares out in light its cry, a slow syllable – no – two syllables, not equal. 'Away' its glaring silence warns. 'Away.'

Past Berwick the fields run to the cliff edge; the flat sea below supports its boats. A trickle of rain down the carriage window swells and subsides and swells and so sticks pulsing in the corner of your eye. Clouds grow like neoplasms on other clouds; the sea moves in its pit; reflections of the firmament conceal the pool's depths. Oilily sliding towards the sea the burn's clean water shines all its bed-stones brown and red. This music comes from inside the river which will teach it to the sea, running with its rainy lessons to the ignorant mother. The sea still nourishes, but coldly now. The Poison Sea folding and ever folding her white hems.

When you come out again through the wide doors of Edinburgh, leaving the clinic in the last week of the year, the earth's shadow has risen in the east and become the early dark. You notice that the stars are out in the clear black afternoon and that for the first time they truly look as if they might have been there all through the day, just a little pale from the sun.

Gravels turn in the wounds that pebbles have made in greater stones and the water's blade cuts them all; but the stones also wound the water, yet you place your hand in the sea and it is not cut off.

It is so new to be human. Let the cells multiply swiftly, prodigal as cancers proliferate in the skull. You know where to stop and you are able to; therefore let the cells replicate in numberless numbers, this useful tumour in the skull's marrow. The modernized brain like an old house with a new verandah. No. Call it a new roof or a second floor, this intelligent rind on old foundations, without a passage or a staircase between, inside or out, not a hatch through. In the new year you will lie down before the professionals as silent as a snake, while they question your ancient brain. Your jaws twitch, but not with speech. There is a taste of blood and bitter leaves.

HEART THROB

─────────── ♡ ───────────

Sara Maitland

Darkness.

A drum roll, distant, muffled within that darkness.

Then half bars of strange music, unformed lost notes, discordant, chaotic, but gentle, solemn, sweet: music from before the dawn of order, pre-creation music. A steady soft drum beat, the pulsing heart of life, but so quiet, so soft that the brain itself must be quieted to hear it. Three beautiful clear notes of a triangle and the darkness begins to shift as coloured smoke wafts dreamily. The high flat mountain comes into focus as pale and far away as the dawn and at the foot of the mountain Kalubini sits, the jewels of his turban catching the refractions of light within the swirling smoke. His face is still, timeless, serious. His knees are flat on the ground while his thighs support his feet in the eternal lotus posture; his palms on his knees are turned outwards and his thumb and index finger form a soft circle within which all the powers of the gods are held.

When there is enough light he begins to move, to gyrate smoothly in strange godlike movements, beyond the power of earth-bound, material bodies. He is snake in its litheness; he is pool of water in its rippled calm; he is frog in its alert stillness; he is palm-tree in its mighty growth; he is power of mind and matter brought together. These are no vulgar contortions, they are the thoughts of a god awakening at dawn in the mystical east and bringing first himself and then the world to light and life.

The music becomes more orderly, fitting itself around the deep heart beat that holds all things together: Kalubini is the heart of the universe. His gentle remote expression never changes as he rises to his feet and moves forward. He looks around, mildly curious, and then smiles. With his smile the light increases. He picks up a small earthenware bowl, plain reddish clay shaped into the inevitable full curve. He holds it between his two long hands, turning it this way and that, peering into its empty roundness. He smiles still, and then murmurs to the bowl. A white dove suddenly, almost shockingly, flies out of it. His expression does not change. He murmurs again. Another dove, very white in the still drifting coloured smoke. The pace of the music quickens almost impercept-ibly, and suddenly there are more and more doves, they flow like a waterfall out of the small round bowl; they rest on Kalubini's turban, on his silken cloak; they peck on the ground. Then all at once in a moment of pure flight they take off together, circle and alight in a small flowering tree which becomes a living rustle of movement, bird and flower together, serene and vital.

Kalubini seems hardly to notice. He fixes his solemn attention on the bowl again and from it now flows, flashing gold and green, a shoal of tiny fish, which he pours gently but steadily into an ornate glass tank near his left hand. When the tank is apparently fuller than it can hold with dancing fish he looks down at his bowl again. For the first time his face assumes an identifiable expression – a wry and amused disappointment. He tosses the bowl aside carelessly and shards of clay tinkle on the ground. He finds another, larger bowl and appears contented with it. Again he turns it slowly in his arms, examining its smooth glazed surface inside and out with apparent disinterest. But when he murmurs to it a cat, pure white and sleek, erupts from the empty space, alights briefly on his shoulder and vanishes. A black dog follows, slim and delicate as a greyhound, tiny as a terrier. It jumps down and curls contentedly at his feet. Kalubini does not smile now but looks infinitely sad. He puts the bowl down on the ground. He whips off his silk cloak and crumples it into the bowl, folding it down until the bowl seems full with it, and then he turns away. Suddenly the heart throb of the drum beat stirs, the silk ripples as though touched by a breeze and begins to rise. From the curved interior of the bowl which did not seem large enough to hold even the little dog a woman emerges, stunningly lovely. Kalubini turns back again and his face is wreathed in delight. He beckons to her and she steps out of the bowl towards him. He raises his right hand imperiously and she starts to dance, her veils parting just enough to show the glittering jewel in her navel and the bright scarlet caste mark in her forehead. Her legs are long and bare, her torso breathtaking, her feet elegant beyond dreaming, her face with its long sloped eyes and perfect mouth is fixed on him and she dances a slow swaying dance of the eternal feminine from the ancient civilisations far over the seas.

The music quickens now and her dance becomes wilder and wilder. She turns from him, dancing away, her eyes fixed on the outside world, on the morning and the space of the universe. It becomes almost a coquettish dance as she realises that there is a whole world to enchant and not just him. Kalubini is furious, he reaches for her but she slips away. He cannot bear it – she has insulted and rejected a god. He leaps upon her, tossing her into the air as though her weight was nothing and his strength infinite. She arches upwards and falls back into his arms, where she lies laughing at him. His anger is the fountain of the world; the calm has vanished from his face and has been replaced by a terror, and awfulness. She realises this and becomes frightened, but he remains stern. He throws her down on a small platform worked with mysterious kabbalistic designs. He covers her again with his cloak and then slams over her a great lacquered lid which he wields as though it was made of straw.

The music stops abruptly. But still he is not content. His fury is manifest in his agitated pacing, in his grinding teeth and in his flashing eyes. With a shocking suddenness he whips out a huge curved sword. He brandishes it wildly, and it slices through the leaves of the tree, fluttering the roosting birds; it slices through the sleeve of his own flowing garment and the shorn silk droops sadly to the ground. After a moment's hesitation he slashes at the lacquered lid and the sword carves through it; then he is hacking, stabbing, chopping in his wrath. From inside comes one painful moan, and a small bleeding hand drops over the edge of the platform. He hurls bits of the lid, bits of his own silk cloak, bits of her veiling across the ground. He is gleeful now and triumphant. He leaps and dances, prances and cavorts in his victory over her.

Abruptly he ceases. He hears a few bars of the music which she had danced to. Suddenly the tiny dog, who has lain peacefully throughout the devastation, lifts up its head and howls. Kalubini is struck; he bends to stroke the dog tenderly and when he raises his head he is weeping. Crystal tears pour from his eyes, but as they fall they turn into jewels, diamonds and pearls, which he gathers in his hands and throws away disgusted. Slowly, sadly, he starts to collect the pieces of his love from where they have fallen. He picks up the little hand and kisses it sorrowfully. He places all the fragments in his bowl. The music starts again. The little dog trots over to the bowl and sits beside it, his head cocked hopefully. Kalubini stands by the bowl murmuring quietly and gently. The coloured smoke begins to move again, the music to settle down, the throbbing of the drum to find its previous rhythm. There is a blinding flash of lightning, a great drum roll of thunder, and there she is! Whole and beautiful as ever. She casts herself into his arms with ecstatic delight. He catches her to his breast and rains god-like kisses upon her. The music reaches a crescendo of excitement; the drum throb, strong and clear now, celebrates the power of life and love. Leaping with joy, tossing her high with easy virility, he carries her away; his face is like a little boy's who got what he wanted for his birthday after all. Vibrant with delight, with no eyes for anything except each other, the couple disappear and only the drum beat continues for another few moments.

It is a terrific act though I say so myself. He's a very skilled illusionist and between us we've managed to pack in almost everything a modern Variety audience wants – oriental mysticism, suspense, a coherent scenario, some effective stunts, a touch of pathos and a bit of implied nooky without passing the boundaries. Managements like it because it doesn't need a cast of thousands and almost every damn theatre in the world can scrape up a mountain scene drop – with our lighting we can pretty much get away with an alpine set if we have to. And, well, I'll tell you what it is, the act has a certain something that really goes over: 'most romantic act in town' some newspaper called it the other day . . . It's what's between the two of us really; whenever we go on, it's there, like a third person in the act, our relationship with each other, and that comes over, a kind of romantic excitement. Neither of us had it before; well, I know I didn't, and I don't think he can have, because as far as the tricks go he hasn't learned anything from me; he is very good; but he

never really made it big. We met two years ago on the
West Coast: I was doing a spot of 'exotic dancing' – well
to be frank I was a call-girl in a honky-tonk with a little
speciality number. He was working what was basically a
parlour act: neat tricks, pretty – especially with the
pigeons and the goldfish, a suave evening-dress conjurer,
with pretensions to class. Not bad. Funny we ever got
together really; we met fooling around at somebody's
place one night, and it just came to us both, the whole
thing. We put the act together on the road coming East. It
went pretty well in Chicago, though it wasn't all fixed
then and we were still having trouble with the music –
before we thought of the drum heart beat to hold it all
together. But by Philadelphia we knew we were on to
something big and managements started knowing it too,
and we were getting good billing and agents after us and
that stuff and New York was just wonderful. We played
Keith's six months straight and we were hot.

Then with the war ending and that let's-go-to-Europe
fever everywhere, and we were both pretty pleased with
ourselves and thought 'Why not? Let's give it a go.'
Berlin, Amsterdam, Paris, London. Two months we've
been playing The Oxford and we don't see much sign of it
coming off yet. So you could say, I would say, that things
were pretty good. In fact there are only two flies in the
ointment. One of them is him and the other is me.

The snag with him is that he's beginning to believe it
all: I think it was that Yoga thing we put in for the
opening, and that crazed teacher he went to, who gave
him all this bit about mystical meditation and oneness
with the universe and the power of the will in harmony
with matter and that stuff. I mean, it is quite impressive
when he puts his ankles over his neck or folds his rib-cage
into accordian pleats, but it's not the key to the universe,
frankly. It doesn't make him a god; it doesn't even make

him a real oriental Indian, for heaven's sake. I mean, the fact that he believes it may help the act, but he can't lay it down when we come off. I should have put my foot down when he first started wearing that damn turban off stage, in public, on the ship coming over, but he told me 'publicity' and 'image' and things, and it was like music to my ears, quite honestly. And where did it leave me? I mean, here I was, for the first time in my life, able to afford a few decent things, and we were in Europe, really classy things I mean, but no, because if he's going to be an Indian then of course I have to be one too, don't I? And Indian women don't go out in public, and Indian women wear saris and veils and keep their mouths shut and just adore their men. And if I argue with him he goes blank on me, his eyes narrow up and his face goes cold and I . . .

Well, I told you there was a snag about me too, and the damn stupid thing is that I've fallen for him. I mean really, the big thing. It's too pathetic, actually: I'm thirty-two years old and I've been around and I wasn't brought up sentimental either. My ma was a tough lady and she always warned me against love and told me straight out what it could do to a woman. And here I am, I'm like a little kid about him. Well, no, not exactly like a little kid, but . . . I don't know how to put it, quite: I never had much schooling and I don't read all the stuff that he reads or know all those lovely words, but he makes me feel. Just that, not good or bad, not happy or sad, but he does make me feel. So much that the feeling is for itself, it doesn't seem to matter what it is. So when his face goes cold or he turns away from me and won't listen or look or touch, then something in me dies. And when he comes back then I'm so happy and grateful that I do anything he wants, anything, anything.

So what with him thinking he's a god, and me thinking he's a god, it's not surprising that three-quarters of the punters end up thinking he's a god too; but for them, of course, it's also just a turn – a classy twenty minutes in the middle of a good variety show and them all snuggled down in the lovely plush seats and afterwards they can just go home.

Well, we go home too, of course, but it doesn't always end there. Of course we were lovers right from the start. Why pay for two beds when you need only pay for one, I said, all bright and brassy, the first week we were on the road. To be honest he wasn't much into it then, I was the one who knew what we were doing, or meant to be doing, just like I was the one pushing the act, shaping it up, you know, because although he's skilful at his own trade he doesn't – or he didn't, anyway – have that feel for a good act that I do. I mean, even when I was just one more little exotic dancer selling something else, I knew, I knew how to put it over. It was when we got the sword trick going, when he got to slash me into little bits twice a night, six nights a week, that things changed. He loved it, he really loved it. And he was wonderful – you could see what it did to him. He took on a new something, a new power with it. And he brought that home to us. He started to change, to take more – to take the lead more, I suppose. And it was wonderful at first. His hands so clever and his body so flexible and I melted for him, I couldn't get enough. He was strong and fit and suddenly he knew exactly what he was doing, and if some of that went a little further than I had expected, well, I found that quite exciting too. He was focussed on me, only me: only I could meet that need in him; he loved me and needed me as much I needed him. We have to be a bit careful, of course, because the costume doesn't cover all that much; but there are things and places, he sucks my blood like a vampire and he needs me to feed him; as he eats me I am eaten by him, I become part of him and . . . Well, of course he would stop if I asked him to, I'm sure he would, I'm pretty nearly damn certain he would; but I don't want him to. And when he's started, of course, it would make him angry if I made him stop, and it would not be fair, because I did lead him on, sexually I mean, I was the one who started it. I need him so much, I need him to stay with me and love me. He's like a god to me, he created me, I owe him so much – I was just a little tart in some San Francisco joint, whose mother had been a hooker and who was going nowhere fast. He made me alive, he made me feel, and all that feeling is for him.

Of course, sometimes when he's out I remember just how bloody stupid it is. What's the point of being half-way across the world if you have to stay in your room the whole time? What's the point of getting top billing and making a fortune if you never see a cent of it? But he comes in and he wants me to be happy and waiting and ready for him, and if I'm not he's so disappointed and knotted up and sad that he can't control himself. It's because he loves me and wants me so much that he gets so angry. I've set his feelings free, he says: before he met me he was all cold, screwed up tight and ungiving, because his mother was a frigid bitch who never gave him any loving, but now I've set all his feelings free, all of them, his loving and his anger and his sadness and his danger, and I must accept them all. Together, he says, we have crashed the barriers of dreary old morality, together we have been set free to understand and enjoy the utter, unutterable beauty of experience. And I know, I know it's true because he has done that for me too. So how can I spit out all my old childish loneliness and jealousy and spite at him, when he takes me in his arms and my belly moves and sings for him, and for him alone. When I know that what we play-act twice nightly before an audience of thousands is true: he took me out of nothing, he destroyed my old life, the old me, he chopped it up in little bits and threw them all away and then he remade me all himself. I do not exist without him. He made me, he can destroy me, that's his right, and it is all right with me.

I don't mind him going out so much, anyway. I don't even like the friends he has now, I don't know them or understand them and they probably wouldn't like me. They're all so fine and fancy, and clever and smart. When we were still in America we went out a lot, especially in New York – we had fun together and good friends. Mostly Vaudeville people, and we were all doing well and there was champagne and parties and a car and decent restaurants and pretty clothes. They were all just people like us, who were suddenly pleased with ourselves and finding the good time after quite a long lot of looking, in some cases. It was lovely, actually; everyone knew who you were really so they didn't mind you pretending to be better than you were, and they were pretending with you.

But after we got to Berlin he started changing. He was an Indian all the time, and he wanted me to be one too. He read mad books at night and started saying he could see the future, started telling me about his powers. He became a stranger and only in bed could I bring him back to me, and only then if I was willing to follow him wherever he wanted to go. He went out late at night drinking absinthe with young men who weren't like us at all. Wild hairy young students and they could talk up a storm. It was quite exciting to listen to at first. I was heady with it, and by all the words they knew and how they treated us – well him, and me with him – as their equals. And they knew so much stuff: poets and thinkers and political writers and strings and strings of wonderful crazy words. They seemed wonderfully romantic to me, though silly too and often rather sweet, though I knew better already than to tell them so. They thought they were so dangerous and splendid. They were delightfully against morality, and I didn't like to tell them they were saying nothing that every pro on the water-front has known for too long and wants to forget. They told him that experience was beautiful, only experience was pure, pure for its own sake. They thought they should prepare themselves for pure experience, for its fullness and its richness, by giving up all the old rules, morality and manners and conventions and stuff; that nothing mattered, that all those things got in the way. I could smile thinking of him and me together in our bed and how that was true and how exciting it was to have thrown away the rules and be in Berlin pretending to be an Indian and getting rich. But I couldn't take them seriously.

Then one night they started asking him about India and his god and his vision of the world and how they could purify themselves and master their emotions through sacrifice and yoga like he did. I started to giggle and he was furious. I thought he would think it was funny, but he didn't see the joke. That's the sort of thing I meant when I said he was starting to believe his whole act. He told me truth was one more convention that had to be set aside, and so was my mockery for the emergence of his true personality. He told me that he was a great Master and that lower beings might need truth but he did not. And he meant it. I was really frightened for a bit – I thought maybe he was cracking up. But the act went on being good, he never put a finger wrong. I should have put my foot down, then and there, but he was so happy and so nice when I agreed with him and so fierce when I didn't. So I didn't. But on the other occasions he would talk of his own friends with so much scorn, so coldly; he would laugh at them and say they were dross for his use, silly fools with words but no wisdom. But they were only foolish little boys.

In Paris, wonderful Paris that I had dreamed of, Paris where I bought lovely dresses and hats that he would not let me wear, in Paris it was more of the same, but different somehow. More spinning words and too much booze, but his friends there took drugs and he did too. And he started to sleep with other women and come home to me and boast about it to me. And worse, somehow, the way he spoke about those women, the way he would mock and jeer at them, talk filth about them to me, foul, disgusting sneering at the poor things. Then he wanted me to sleep with other men and tell him about them; he wanted me to do things with other men, and other women, and have him watch us. When I said it was wrong he hit me – not for fun, not for sex, but hard cold in anger; it was the first time he had ever done that. He knocked me to the floor and stood over me and said there was slave morality and Master morality and if I chose to be a slave he would treat me like one, but if I wanted to be a free spirit I must obey him. I told him I couldn't help my natural feelings and he stood over me, tall and beautiful, and he said, and I can remember it clearly, he said natural feelings were only there to challenge the striving soul. 'I am showing you the Superman,' he said sternly. 'Natural man is something that can be overcome, that must be surpassed.' And I was so frightened and so crazy for him and he was so completely filled up with his own power that I said I wanted to be his slave, the slave girl of the new Superman, and he smiled. I thought about running away then, when I said it, and bloody well should have too. After that it was too late. Once I had accepted his smile, consented to it and to what followed that smile; once I had learned how far he was prepared to go with my body and how I was prepared to follow him there, how I could love what he did to me and cry out for more, then there was no place to run. He was my whole world.

Without him I did not exist. I love him most terribly.

And here in London, well, I don't see him much after the show. Late at night, in the early foggy mornings of London city, he comes in wild and hectic. I wait for him, sometimes all night, long past any desire to sleep, I wait for his hands and his teeth and his tongue to come to me and make me alive again, to take away the fear and the loneliness, to make me real, to make me feel. Occasionally his friends will come to the dressing room between the shows. Last night a long thin woman came; and she bowed low over his hand and called him Master and Guru. He smiled at her with infinite cold distance. I suppose I should have been glad of the distance. She petted me like I pet our little dog. She told me I was lucky to share my life with the life of the greatest spiritual master of our generation, but she was not speaking to me. She was speaking to him. He smiled. She smiled. As she left she reminded him, with caressing veneration, that she would see him later and was looking forward to a further display of his mystic powers. But that time she was talking to me and not to him.

And after she had gone I was glad that he hit me, that he beat me carefully and systematically where it hurt most and showed least, because it still meant that he needed me for something, just like I needed him.

Last night he raged on about the Superman. He told me that to find greatness a man must commit himself completely to his worldly goals, that he must be prepared to sacrifice life itself for them, and that out of the rubble, the ashes, the chaos of that destruction, that sacrifice, the Superman, the new all-powerful master of the universe, would arise. Then he went out and did not return all night.

And suddenly I knew, what I had in fact known all along, known ever since we came to Europe. I will be the sacrifice. One day, one evening under the glow of the stage lights he will cover me with the cloak and the lacquer lid and he will, in front of a breathless audience, a doting venerating crowd, he will cut me up into little bits with his long curved sword. He will be ecstatic while he does it. And the funny thing is so will I. I won't roll away off the little table as I'm meant to do, slipping out under the concealed flap and dropping the dummy hand as I go. I'll take it, proud and happy and sexy. It will be wonderful. He will be the most powerful man in the world for that moment. He'll be the big star of the season. Their horror will be his ultimate reward and mine too. I'm the showman of this team and I always have been. It will be an unforgettable night at the theatre, I can tell you. And I don't mind too much, to tell the truth, because there is not much else left for me, and because I'm the only woman in the world he could do that to. I just want to let everyone else know first, because there's a bit of me, brought up to be a competent and capable hooker, who knows perfectly well that the whole thing is bloody stupid.

I don't know which night it will be. That's part of the magic.

But it will happen, one night.

I know. He knows I know. We have both known for quite a long time.

That is the extraordinary extra something that goes on stage with us each night. That's why the papers call it the 'most romantic act in town.'

It's a terrific act, though I say so myself.

BIG BERTHA STORIES

♡

Bobbie Ann Mason

Donald is home again, laughing and singing. He comes home from Central City, Kentucky, near the strip mines, only when he feels like it, like an absentee landlord checking on his property. He is always in such a good humor when he returns that Jeannette forgives him. She cooks for him – ugly, pasty things she gets with food stamps. Sometimes he brings steaks and ice cream, occasionally money. Rodney, their child, hides in the closet when he arrives, and Donald goes around the house talking loudly about the little boy named Rodney who used to live there – the one who fell into a septic tank, or the one stolen by Gypsies. The stories change. Rodney usually stays in the closet until he has to pee, and then he hugs his father's knees, forgiving him, just as Jeannette does. The way Donald saunters through the door, swinging a six-pack of beer, with a big grin on his face, takes her breath away. He leans against the door facing, looking sexy in his baseball cap and his shaggy red beard and his sunglasses. He wears sunglasses to be like the Blues Brothers, but he in no way resembles either of the Blues Brothers. I should have my head examined, Jeannette thinks.

The last time Donald was home, they went to the shopping center to buy Rodney some shoes advertised on sale. They stayed at the shopping center half the

35

afternoon, just looking around. Donald and Rodney played video games. Jeannette felt they were a normal family. Then, in the parking lot, they stopped to watch a man on a platform demonstrating snakes. Children were petting a twelve-foot python coiled around the man's shoulders. Jeannette felt faint.

'Snakes won't hurt you unless you hurt them,' said Donald as Rodney stroked the snake.

'It feels like chocolate,' he said.

The snake man took a tarantula from a plastic box and held it lovingly in his palm. He said, 'If you drop a tarantula, it will shatter like a Christmas ornament.'

'I hate this,' said Jeannette.

'Let's get out of here,' said Donald.

Jeannette felt her family disintegrating like a spider shattering as Donald hurried them away from the shopping center. Rodney squalled and Donald dragged him along. Jeannette wanted to stop for ice cream. She wanted them all to sit quietly together in a booth, but Donald rushed them to the car, and he drove them home in silence, his face growing grim.

'Did you have bad dreams about the snakes?' Jeannette asked Rodney the next morning at breakfast. They were eating pancakes made with generic pancake mix. Rodney slapped his fork in the pond of syrup on his pancakes. 'The black racer is the farmer's friend,' he said soberly, repeating a fact learned from the snake man.

'Big Bertha kept black racers,' said Donald. 'She trained them for the 500.' Donald doesn't tell Rodney ordinary children's stories. He tells him a series of strange stories he makes up about Big Bertha. Big Bertha is what he calls the huge strip-mining machine in Muhlenberg County, but he has Rodney believing that Big Bertha is a female version of Paul Bunyan.

'Snakes don't run in the 500,' said Rodney.

'This wasn't the Indy 500, or the Daytona 500, none of your well-known 500s,' said Donald. 'This was the Possum Trot 500, and it was a long time ago. Big Bertha started the original 500 with snakes. Black racers and blue racers mainly. Also some red-and-white striped racers, but those are rare.'

'We always ran for the hoe if we saw a black racer,' Jeannette said, remembering her childhood in the country.

In a way, Donald's absences are a fine arrangement, even considerate. He is sparing them his darkest moods, when he can't cope with his memories of Vietnam. Vietnam had never seemed such a meaningful fact until a couple of years ago, when he grew depressed and moody, and then he started going away to Central City. He frightened Jeannette, and she always said the wrong thing in her efforts to soothe him. If the welfare people find out he is spending occasional weekends at home, and even bringing some money, they will cut off her assistance. She applied for welfare because she can't depend on him to send money, but she knows he blames her for losing faith in him. He isn't really working regularly at the strip mining. He is mostly just hanging around there, watching the land being scraped away, trees coming down, bushes flung in the air. Sometimes he operates a steam shovel, and when he comes home his clothes are filled with the clay and it is caked on his shoes. The clay is the color of butterscotch pudding.

At first, he tried to explain to Jeannette. He said, 'If we could have had tanks over there as big as Big Bertha, we wouldn't have lost the war. Strip mining is just like what we were doing over there. We were stripping off the top. The topsoil is like the culture and the people, the best part of the land and the country. America was just stripping off the top, the best. We ruined it. Here, at least the coal companies have to plant vetch and loblolly pines and all kinds of trees and bushes. If we'd done that in Vietnam, maybe we'd have left that country in better shape.'

'Wasn't Vietnam a long time ago?' Jeannette asked.

She didn't want to hear about Vietnam. She thought it was unhealthy to dwell on it so much. He should live in the present. Her mother is afraid Donald will do something violent, because she once read in the newspaper that a veteran in Louisville held his little girl hostage in their apartment until he had a shootout with the police and was killed. But Jeannette can't imagine Donald doing anything so extreme. When she first met him, several years ago, at her parents' pit-barbecue luncheonette, where she was working then, he had a good job at a lumberyard and he dressed nicely. He took her out to eat at a fancy restaurant. They got plastered and ended up in a motel in Tupelo, Mississippi on Elvis Presley Boulevard. Back then, he talked nostalgically about his years in Vietnam, about how beautiful it was, how different the people were. He could never seem to explain what he meant. 'They're just different,' he said.

They went riding around in a yellow 1957 Chevy convertible. He drives too fast now, but he didn't then, maybe because he was so protective of the car. It was a classic. He sold it three years ago and made a good profit. About the time he sold the Chevy, his moods began changing, his even-tempered nature shifting, like driving on a smooth interstate and then switching to a secondary road. He had headaches and bad dreams. But his nightmares seemed trivial. He dreamed of riding a train through the Rocky Mountains, of hijacking a plane to Cuba, of stringing up barbed wire around the house. He dreamed he lost a doll. He got drunk and rammed the car, the Chevy's successor, into a Civil War statue in front of the courthouse. When he got depressed over the meaninglessness of his job, Jeannette felt guilty about spending money on something nice for the house, and she tried to make him feel his job had meaning by reminding him that, after all, they had a child to think of. 'I don't like his name,' Donald said once. 'What a stupid name. Rodney. I never did like it.'

Rodney has dreams about Big Bertha, echoes of his father's nightmare, like TV cartoon versions of Donald's memories of the war. But Rodney loves the stories, even though they are confusing, with lots of ends. The latest in the Big Bertha series is 'Big Bertha and the Neutron Bomb.' Last week it was 'Big Bertha and the MX Missile.' In the new story, Big Bertha takes a trip to California to go surfing with Big Mo, her male counterpart. On the beach, corn dogs and snow cones are free and the surfboards turn into dolphins. Everyone is having fun until the neutron bomb comes. Rodney loves the part where everyone keels over dead. Donald acts it out, collapsing on the rug. All the dolphins and the surfers keel over, everyone except Big Bertha. Big Bertha is so big she is immune to the neutron bomb.

'Those stories aren't true,' Jeannette tells Rodney.

Rodney staggers and falls down on the rug, his arms and legs akimbo. He gets the giggles and can't stop. When his spasms finally subside, he says, 'I told Scottie Bidwell about Big Bertha and he didn't believe me.'

Donald picks Rodney up under the armpits and sets him upright. 'You tell Scottie Bidwell if he saw Big Bertha he would pee in his pants on the spot, he would be so impressed.'

'Are you scared of Big Bertha?'

'No, I'm not. Big Bertha is just like a wonderful woman, a big fat woman who can sing the blues. Have you ever heard heard Big Mama Thornton?'

'No.'

'Well, Big Bertha's like her, only she's the size of a tall building. She's slow as a turtle, and when she crosses the road they have to reroute traffic. She's big enough to straddle a four-lane highway. She's so tall she can see all the way to Tennessee, and when she belches, there's a tornado. She's really something. She can even fly.'

'She's too big to fly,' Rodney says doubtfully. He makes a face like a wadded-up washrag and Donald wrestles him to the floor again.

Donald has been drinking all evening, but he isn't drunk. The ice cubes melt and he pours the drink out and refills it. He keeps on talking. Jeannette cannot remember him talking so much about the war. He is telling her about an ammunitions dump. Jeannette had the vague idea that an ammo dump is a mound of shotgun shells, heaps of cartridge casings and bomb shells, or whatever is left over, a vast waste pile from the war, but Donald says that is wrong. He has spent an hour describing it in detail, so that she will understand.

He refills the glass with ice, some 7-Up, and a shot of Jim Beam. He slams doors and drawers, looking for a compass. Jeannette can't keep track of the conversation. It doesn't matter that her hair is uncombed and her lipstick eaten away. He isn't seeing her.

'I want to draw the compound for you,' he says, sitting down at the table with a sheet of Rodney's tablet paper.

Donald draws the map in red-and-blue ballpoint, with asterisks and technical labels that mean nothing to her. He draws some circles with the compass and measures some angles. He makes a red dot on an oblique line, a path that leads to the ammo dump.

'That's where I was. Right there,' he says. 'There was a water buffalo that tripped a land mine and its horn just

40

flew off and stuck in the wall of the barracks like a machete thrown back-handed.' He puts a dot where the land mine was, and he doodles awhile with the red ballpoint pen, scribbling something on the edge of the map that looks like feathers. 'The dump was here and I was there and over there was where we piled the sandbags. And here were the tanks.' He draws tanks, a row of squares with handles – guns sticking out.

'Why are you going to so much trouble to tell me about a buffalo horn that got stuck in a wall?' she wants to know.

But Donald just looks at her as though she has asked something obvious.

'Maybe I *could* understand if you'd let me,' she says cautiously.

'You could never understand.' He draws another tank.

In bed, it is the same as it has been since he started going away to Central City – the way he claims his side of the bed, turning away from her. Tonight, she reaches for him and he lets her be close to him. She cries for a while and he lies there, waiting for her to finish, as though she were merely putting on make-up.

'Do you want me to tell you a Big Bertha story?' he asks playfully.

'You act like you're in love with Big Bertha.'

He laughs, breathing on her. But he won't come closer.

'You don't care what I look like anymore,' she says. 'What am I supposed to think?'

'There's nobody else. There's not anybody but you.'

Loving a giant machine is incomprehensible to Jeannette. There must be another woman, someone that large in his mind. Jeannette has seen the strip-mining machine. The top of the crane is visible beyond a rise along the Western Kentucky Parkway. The strip mining is kept just out of sight of travelers because it would give

41

them a poor image of Kentucky.

For three weeks, Jeannette has been seeing a psychologist at the free mental health clinic. He's a small man from out of state. His name is Dr Robinson, but she calls him The Rapist, because the word *therapist* can be divided into two words, *the rapist*. He doesn't think her joke is clever, and he acts as though he has heard it a thousand times before. He has a habit of saying, 'Go with that feeling,' the same way Bob Newhart did on his old TV show. It's probably the first lesson in the textbook, Jeannette thinks.

She told him about Donald's last days on his job at the lumberyard – how he let the stack of lumber fall deliberately and didn't know why, and about how he went away soon after that, and how the Big Bertha stories started. Dr Robinson seems to be waiting for her to make something out of it all, but it's maddening that he won't tell her what to do. After three visits, Jeannette has grown angry with him, and now she's holding back things. She won't tell him whether Donald slept with her or not when he came home last. Let him guess, she thinks.

'Talk about yourself,' he says.

'What about me?'

'You speak so vaguely about Donald that I get the feeling that you see him as somebody larger than life. I can't quite picture him. That makes me wonder what that says about you.' He touches the end of his tie to his nose and sniffs it.

When Jeannette suggests that she bring Donald in, the therapist looks bored and says nothing.

'He had another nightmare when he was home last,' Jeannette says. 'He dreamed he was crawling through tall grass and people were after him.'

'How do *you* feel about that?' The Rapist asks eagerly.

'I didn't have the nightmare,' she says coldly. 'Donald

42

did. I came to you to get advice about Donald, and you're acting like I'm the one who's crazy. I'm not crazy. But I'm lonely.'

Jeannette's mother, behind the counter of the luncheonette, looks lovingly at Rodney pushing buttons on the jukebox in the corner. 'It's a shame about that youngun,' she says tearfully. 'That boy needs a daddy.'

'What are you trying to tell me? That I should file for divorce and get Rodney a new daddy?'

Her mother looks hurt. 'No, honey,' she says. 'You need to get Donald to seek the Lord. And you need to pray more. You haven't been going to church lately.'

'Have some barbecue,' Jeannette's father booms, as he comes in from the back kitchen. 'And I want you to take a pound home with you. You've got a growing boy to feed.'

'I want to take Rodney to church,' Mama says. 'I want to show him off, and it might do some good.'

'People will think he's an orphan,' Dad says.

'I don't care,' Mama says. 'I just love him to pieces and I want to take him to church. Do you care if I take him to church, Jeannette?'

'No. I don't care if you take him to church.' She takes the pound of barbecue from her father. Grease splotches the brown wrapping paper. Dad has given them so much barbecue that Rodney is burned out on it and won't eat it anymore.

Jeannette wonders if she would file for divorce if she could get a job. It is a thought – for the child's sake, she thinks. But there aren't many jobs around. With the cost of a babysitter, it doesn't pay her to work. When Donald first went away, her mother kept Rodney and she had a good job, waitressing at a steak house, but the steak house burned down one night – a grease fire in the kitchen. After that, she couldn't find a steady job, and she was reluctant to ask her mother to keep Rodney again because of her bad hip. At the steak house, men gave her tips and left their telephone numbers on the bill when they paid. They tucked dollar bills and notes in the pockets of her apron. One note said, 'I want to hold your muffins.' They were real-estate developers and business-men on important missions for the Tennessee Valley Authority. They were boisterous and they drank too much. They said they'd take her for a cruise on the *Delta Queen*, but she didn't believe them. She knew how expensive that was. They talked about their speedboats and invited her for rides on Lake Barkley, or for spins in their private planes. They always used the word *spin*. The idea made her dizzy. Once, Jeannette let an electronics salesman take her for a ride in his Cadillac, and they breezed down The Trace, the wilderness road that winds down the Land Between the Lakes. His car had automatic windows and a stereo system and lighted computer-screen numbers on the dash that told him how many miles to the gallon he was getting and other statistics. He said the numbers distracted him and he had almost had several wrecks. At the restaurant, he had been flamboyant, admired by his companions. Alone with Jeannette in the Cadillac, on The Trace, he was shy and awkward, and really not very interesting. The most interesting thing about him, Jeannette thought, was all the lighted numbers on his dashboard. The Cadillac had everything but video games. But she'd rather be riding around with Donald, no matter where they ended up.

While the social worker is there, filling out her report, Jeannette listens for Donald's car. When the social worker drove up, the flutter and wheeze of her car sounded like

Donald's old Chevy, and for a moment Jeannette's mind lapsed back in time. Now she listens, hoping he won't drive up. The social worker is younger than Jeannette and has been to college. Her name is Miss Bailey, and she's excessively cheerful, as though in her line of work she has seen hardships that make Jeannette's troubles seem like a trip to Hawaii.

'Is your little boy still having those bad dreams?' Miss Bailey asks, looking up from her clipboard.

Jeannette nods and looks at Rodney, who has his finger in his mouth and won't speak.

'Has the cat got your tongue?' Miss Bailey asks.

'Show her your pictures, Rodney.' Jeannette explains, 'He won't talk about the dreams, but he draws pictures of them.'

Rodney brings his tablet of pictures and flips through them silently. Miss Bailey says, 'Hmm.' They are stark line drawings, remarkably steady lines for his age. 'What is this one?' she asks. 'Let me guess. Two scoops of ice cream?'

The picture is two huge circles, filling the page, with three tiny stick people in the corner.

'These are Big Bertha's titties,' says Rodney.

Miss Bailey chuckles and winks at Jeannette. 'What do you like to read, hon?' she asks Rodney.

'Nothing.'

'He can read,' says Jeannette. 'He's smart.'

'Do you like to read?' Miss Bailey asks Jeannette. She glances at the pile of paperbacks on the coffee table. She is probably going to ask where Jeannette got the money for them.

'I don't read,' says Jeannette. 'If I read, I just go crazy.'

When she told The Rapist she couldn't concentrate on anything serious, he said she read romance novels in order to escape from reality. 'Reality, hell!' she had said.

'Reality's my whole problem.'

'It's too bad Rodney's not here,' Donald is saying. Rodney is in the closet again. 'Santa Claus has to take back all these toys. Rodney would love this bicycle! And this Pac-Man game. Santa has to take back so many things he'll have to have a pickup truck!'

'You didn't bring him anything. You never bring him anything,' says Jeannette.

He has brought doughnuts and dirty laundry. The clothes he is wearing are caked with clay. His beard is lighter from working out in the sun, and he looks his usual joyful self, the way he always is before his moods take over, like migraine headaches, which some people describe as storms.

Donald coaxes Rodney out of the closet with the doughnuts.

'Were you a good boy this week?'

'I don't know.'

'I hear you went to the shopping center and showed out.' It is not true that Rodney made a big scene. Jeannette has already explained that Rodney was upset because she wouldn't buy him an Atari. But she didn't blame him for crying. She was tired of being unable to buy him anything.

Rodney eats two doughnuts and Donald tells him a long, confusing story about Big Bertha and a rock-and-roll band. Rodney interrupts him with dozens of questions. In the story, the rock-and-roll band gives a concert in a place that turns out to be a toxic-waste dump and the contamination is spread all over the country. Big Bertha's solution to this problem is not at all clear. Jeannette stays in the kitchen, trying to think of something original to do with instant potatoes and leftover barbecue.

'We can't go on like this,' she says that evening in bed.

'We're just hurting each other. Something has to change.'

He grins like a kid. 'Coming home from Muhlenberg County is like R and R – rest and recreation. I explain that in case you think R and R means rock-and-roll. Or maybe rumps and rears. Or rust and rot.' He laughs and draws a circle in the air with his cigarette.

'I'm not that dumb.'

'When I leave, I go back to the mines.' He sighs, as though the mines were some eternal burden.

Her mind skips ahead to the future: Donald locked away somewhere, coloring in a coloring book and making clay pots, her and Rodney in some other town, with another man – someone dull and not at all sexy. Summoning up her courage, she says, 'I haven't been through what you've been through and maybe I don't have a right to say this, but sometimes I think you act superior because you went to Vietnam, like nobody can ever know what you know. Well, maybe not. But you've still got your legs, even if you don't know what to do with what's between them anymore.' Bursting into tears of apology, she can't help adding, 'You can't go on telling Rodney those awful stories. He has nightmares when you're gone.'

Donald rises from bed and grabs Rodney's picture from the dresser, holding it as he might have held a hand grenade. 'Kids betray you,' he says, turning the picture in his hand.

'If you cared about him, you'd stay here.' As he sets the picture down, she asks, 'What can I do? How can I understand what's going on in your mind? Why do you go there? Strip mining's bad for the ecology and you don't have any business strip mining.'

'My job is serious, Jeannette. I run that steam shovel and put the topsoil back on. I'm reclaiming the land.' He keeps talking, in a gentler voice, about strip mining, the

47

same old things she has heard before, comparing Big
Bertha to a supertank. If only they had had Big Bertha in
Vietnam. He says, 'When they strip off the top, I keep
looking for those tunnels where the Viet Cong hid. They
had so many tunnels it was unbelievable. Imagine
Mammoth Cave going all the way across Kentucky.'

'Mammoth Cave's one of the natural wonders of the
world,' says Jeannette brightly. She is saying the wrong
thing again.

At the kitchen table at 2 a.m., he's telling about C-5A's. A
C-5A is so big it can carry troops and tanks and
helicopters, but it's not big enough to hold Big Bertha.
Nothing could hold Big Bertha. He rambles on, and when
Jeannette shows him Rodney's drawing of the circles,
Donald smiles. Dreamily, he begins talking about
women's breasts and thighs – the large, round thighs and
big round breasts of American women, contrasted with
the frail, delicate beauty of the Orientals. It is like
comparing oven broilers and banties, he says. Jeannette
relaxes. A confession about another lover from long ago
is not so hard to take. He seems stuck on the breasts and
thighs of American women – insisting that she understand
how small and delicate the Orientals are, but then he
abruptly returns to tanks and helicopters.

'A Bell Huey Cobra – my God, what a beautiful
machine. So efficient!' Donald takes the food processor
blade from the drawer where Jeannette keeps it. He says,
'A rotor blade from a chopper could just slice anything to
bits.'

'Don't do that,' Jeannette says.

He is trying to spin the blade on the counter, like a top.
'Here's what would happen when a chopper blade hits a
power line – not many of those over there! – or a tree.
Not many trees, either, come to think of it, after all the

48

Agent Orange.' He drops the blade and it glances off the open drawer and falls to the floor, spiking the vinyl.

At first, Jeannette thinks the screams are hers, but they are his. She watches him cry. She has never seen anyone cry so hard, like an intense summer thundersower. All she knows to do is shove Kleenex at him. Finally, he is able to say, 'You thought I was going to hurt you. That's why I'm crying.'

'Go ahead and cry,' Jeannette says, holding him close. 'Don't go away.'

'I'm right here. I'm not going anywhere.'

In the night, she still listens, knowing his monologue is being burned like a tattoo into her brain. She will never forget it. His voice grows soft and he plays with a ballpoint pen, jabbing holes in a paper towel. Bullet holes, she thinks. His beard is like a bird's nest, woven with dark corn silks.

'This is just a story,' he says, 'Don't mean nothing. Just relax.' She is sitting on the hard edge of the kitchen chair, her toes cold on the floor, waiting. His tears have dried up and left a slight catch in his voice.

'We were in a big camp near a village. It was pretty routine and kind of soft there for a while. Now and then we'd go into Da Nang and whoop it up. We had been in the jungle for several months, so the two months at this village was a sort of rest — an R and R almost. Don't shiver. This is just a little story. Don't mean nothing! This is nothing, compared to what I could tell you. Just listen. We lost our fear. At night there would be some incoming and we'd see these tracers in the sky, like shooting stars up close, but it was all pretty minor and we didn't take it seriously, after what we'd been through. In the village I knew this Vietnamese family — a woman and her two daughters. They sold Cokes and beer to GIs. The oldest daughter was named Phan. She could speak a little English. She was really smart. I used to get see them in their hooch in the afternoons – in the siesta time of day. It was so hot there. Phan was beautiful, like the country. The village was ratty, but the country was pretty. And she was beautiful, just like she had grown up out of the jungle, like one of those flowers that bloomed high up in the trees and freaked us out sometimes, thinking it was a sniper. She was so gentle, with these eyes shaped like peach pits, and she was no bigger than a child of maybe 13 or 14. I felt funny about her size at first, but later it didn't matter. It was just some wonderful feature about her, like a woman's hair, or her breasts.'

He stops and listens, the way they used to listen for crying sounds when Rodney was a baby. He says, 'She'd take those big banana leaves and fan me while I lay there in the heat.'

'I didn't know they had bananas over there.'

'There's a lot you don't know! Listen! Phan was twenty-three, and her brothers were off fighting. I never even asked which side they were fighting on.' He laughs. 'She got a kick out of the word *fan*. I told her that *fan* was the same word as her name. She thought I meant her name was banana. In Vietnamese the same word can have a dozen different meanings, depending on your tone of voice. I bet you didn't know, that did you?'

'No. What happened to her?'

'I don't know.'

'Is that the end of the story?'

'I don't know.' Donald pauses, then goes on talking about the village, the girl, the banana leaves, talking in a monotone that is making Jeannette's flesh crawl. He could be the news radio from the next room.

'You must have really liked that place. Do you wish you could go back there to find out what happened to her?'

'It's not there anymore,' he says. 'It blew up.'

Donald abruptly goes to the bathroom. She hears the water running, the pipes in the basement shaking.

'It was so pretty,' he says when he returns. He rubs his elbow absent-mindedly. 'That jungle was the most beautiful place in the world. You'd have thought you were in paradise. But we blew it sky-high.'

In her arms, he is shaking, like the pipes in the basement, which are still vibrating. Then the pipes let go, after a long shudder, but he continues to tremble.

They are driving to the Veterans Hospital. It was Donald's idea. She didn't have to persuade him. When she made up the bed that morning – with a finality that shocked her, as though she knew they wouldn't be in it again together – he told her it would be like R and R. Rest was what he needed. Neither of them had slept at all during the night. Jeannette felt she had to stay awake, to listen for more.

'Talk about strip mining,' she says now. 'That's what they'll do to your head. They'll dig out all those ugly memories, I hope. We don't need them around here.' She pats his knee.

It is a cloudless day, not the setting for this sober journey. She drives and Donald goes along obediently, with the resignation of an old man being taken to a rest home. They are driving through southern Illinois, known as Little Egypt, for some obscure reason Jeannette has never understood. Donald still talks, but very quietly, without urgency. When he points out the scenery, Jeannette thinks of the early days of their marriage, when they would take a drive like this and laugh hysterically. Now Jeannette points out funny things they see. The Little Egypt Hot Dog World, Pharaoh Cleaners, Pyramid

Body Shop. She is scarcely aware that she is driving, and when she sees a sign, Little Egypt Starlite Club, she is confused for a moment, wondering where she has been transported.

As they part, he asks, 'What will you tell Rodney if I don't come back? What if they keep me here indefinitely?'

'You're coming back. I'm telling him you're coming back soon.'

'Tell him I went off with Big Bertha. Tell him she's taking me on a sea cruise, to the South Sea.'

'No. You can tell him that yourself.'

He starts singing a jumpy tune, 'Won't you let me take you on a sea cruise?' He grins at her and pokes her in the ribs.

'You're coming back,' she says.

Donald writes from the VA Hospital, saying that he is making progress. They are running tests, and he meets in a therapy group in which all the veterans trade memories. Jeannette is no longer on welfare because she now has a job waitressing at Fred's Family Restaurant. She waits on families, waits for Donald to come home so they can come here and eat together like a family. The fathers look at her with downcast eyes, and the children throw food. While Donald is gone, she rearranges the furniture. She reads some books from the library. She does a lot of thinking. It occurs to her that even though she loved him, she has thought of Donald primarily as a husband, a provider, someone whose name she shared, the father of her child, someone like the fathers who come to the Wednesday night all-you-can-eat fish fry. She hasn't thought of him as himself. She wasn't brought up that way, to examine someone's soul. When it comes to something deep inside, nobody will take it out and examine it, the way they will look at clothing in a store for flaws in the manufacturing. She tries to explain all this to The Rapist, and he says she's looking better, got sparkle in her eyes. 'Big deal,' says Jeannette. 'Is that all you can say?'

She takes Rodney to the shopping center, their favorite thing to do together, even though Rodney always begs to buy something. They got to Penney's perfume counter. There, she usually hits a sample bottle of cologne – Chantilly or Charlie or something strong. Today she hits two or three and comes out of Penney's smelling like a flower garden.

'You stink!' Rodney cries, wrinkling his nose like a rabbit.

'Big Bertha smells like this, only a thousand times worse, she's so big,' says Jeannette impulsively. 'Didn't Daddy tell you that?'

'Daddy's a messenger from the devil.'

This is an idea he must have gotten from church. Her parents have been taking him every Sunday. When Jeannette tries to reassure him about his father, Rodney is skeptical. 'He gets that funny look on his face like he can see through me,' the child says.

'Something's missing,' Jeannette says with a rush of optimism, a feeling of recognition. 'Something happened to him once and took out the part that shows how much he cares about us.'

'The way we had the cat fixed?'

'I guess. Something like that.' The appropriateness of his remark stuns her, as though, in a way, her child has understood Donald all along. Rodney's pictures have been more peaceful lately, pictures of skinny trees and airplanes flying low. This morning he drew pictures of tall grass, with creatures hiding in it. The grass is tilted at an angle, as though a light breeze is blowing through it.

With her paycheck, Jeannette buys Rodney a present, a

miniature trampoline they have seen advertised on television. It is called Mr Bouncer. Rodney is thrilled about the trampoline, and he jumps on it until his face is red. Jeannette discovers that she enjoys it, too. She puts it out on the grass, and they take turns jumping. She has an image of herself on the trampoline, her sailor collar flapping at the moment when Donald returns and sees her flying. One day a neighbor driving by slows downs and calls out to Jeannette as she is bouncing on the trampoline, 'You'll tear your insides loose!' Jeannette starts thinking about that, and the idea is so horrifying she stops jumping so much. That night, she has a nightmare about the trampoline. In her dream, she is jumping on soft moss, and then it turns into a springy pile of dead bodies.

DOWN THE CLINICAL DISCO

♡

Fay Weldon

You never know where you'll meet your own true love. I met mine down the clinical disco. That's him over there, the thin guy with the jeans, the navy jumper and the red woolly cap. He looks pretty much like anyone else, don't you think? That's hard work on his part, not to mention mine, but we got there in the end. Do you want a drink? Gin? Tonic? Fine. I'll just have an orange juice. I don't drink. Got to be careful. You never know who's watching. They're everywhere. Sorry, forget I said that. Even a joke can be paranoia. Do you like my hair? That's a golden gloss rinse. Not my style really: I have this scar down my cheek, see: if I turn to the light? A good short crop is what suits me best, always was: I suppose I've got what you'd call a strong face. Oops, sorry, dear, didn't mean to spill your gin; it's the heels, I do my best but I can never quite manage stilettos. But it's an ill wind; anyone watching would think I'm ever so slightly tipsy, and that's normal, isn't it? It is not absolutely A-okay not to drink alcohol. On the obsessive side. *Darling, of course there are people watching.*

Let me tell you about the clinical disco while Eddie finishes his game of darts. He hates darts but darts are what men do in pubs, okay? The clincal disco is what they have once a month at Broadmoor. (Yes, that place. Broadmoor. The secure hospital for the criminally

55

insane.) You didn't know they had women there? They do. One woman to every nine men. They often don't look all that like women when they go in, but they sure as hell look like them when (and if, if, if, if, if, if, if) they go out.

How did I get to be in there? You really want to know? I'd been having this crummy time at home and this crummy time at work. I was married to this guy I loved, God knows why, in retrospect, but I did, only he fancied my mother, and he got her pregnant – while I was out at work – did you know women can get pregnant at fifty? He didn't, she didn't, I didn't – but she was! My mum said he only married me to be near her anyway and I was the one ought to have an abortion. So I did. It went wrong and messed me up inside, so I couldn't have babies, and my mum said what did it matter, I was a lesbian anyway, just look at me. I got the scar in a road accident, in case you're wondering. And I thought what the hell, who wants a man, who wants a mother, and walked out on them. And I was working at the Royal Opera House for this man who was a real pain, and you know how these places get: the dramas and the rows and the overwork and the underpay and the show must go on, though you're dropping dead. Dropping dead babies. No, I'm not crying. What do you think I am, a depressive! I'm as normal as the next person.

What I did was set fire to the office. Just an impulse. I was having these terrible pains and he made me work late. He said it was my fault Der Rosenkavalier's wig didn't fit. He said I'd made his opera house an international laughing stock: it slipped and the *New York Times* jeered. But it wasn't my fault about the wig: wardrobe had put the message through to props, not administration. And I sat in front of the VDU – the union are against them: they cause infertility in women but what employer's going to bother about a thing like that – they prefer everyone childless any day – and thought about my husband and my mum, five months pregnant, and lit a cigarette. I'd given up smoking for a whole year but this business at home had made me start again. Have you ever had an abortion at five months? No? Not many have.

How's your drink? How's Eddie getting on with the darts? Started another game? That's A-okay, that's fine by me, that's normal.

So what were we saying, Linda? Oh yes, arson. That's what they called it. I just moved my cigarette lighter under the curtains and they went up, whoosh, and that caught some kind of soundproof ceiling in-fill they use these days instead of plaster. Up it all went. Whoosh again. Four hundred pounds' worth of damage. Or so they said. If you ask me, they were glad of the excuse to redecorate.

Like a fool, instead of lying and just saying it was an accident, I said I'd done it on purpose, I was glad I had, opera was a waste of public funds, and working late a waste of my life. That was before I got to court. The solicitor laddie warned me off. He said arson was no laughing matter, they came down very hard on arson. I thought a fine, perhaps: he said no, prison. Years not months.

You know, my mum didn't even come to the hearing? She had a baby girl. I thought there might be something wrong with it, my mum being so old, but there wasn't. Perhaps the father being so young made up for it.

There was a barrister chappie, he said, look you've been upset, you are upset, all this business at home, the thing for you to do is plead insane; we'll get you sent to Broadmoor, it's the best place in the country for psychiatric care, they'll have you right in the head in no time. Otherwise it's Holloway, and that's all strip cells and major tranquillisers, and not so much a short sharp shock as a long sharp shock. Years, it could be, arson.

So that's what I did, I pleaded insane, and got an indefinite sentence, which meant into Broadmoor until such time as I was cured and safe to be let out into the world again. I never was unsafe. You know what one of those famous opera singers said when she heard what I'd done? 'Good for Philly,' she said. 'Best thing that could possibly happen: the whole place razed to the ground!' Only of course it wasn't even razed to the ground, just one room already in need of redecoration slightly blackened. When did I realise I'd made a mistake? The minute I saw Broadmoor: a great black pile: the second I got into this reception room. There were three women nurses in there, standing around a bath of hot water; great hefty women and male nurses too, and they were talking and laughing. Well, not exactly laughing, an Inside equivalent, a sort of heavy grunting ha-ha-ha they manage, half way between sex and hate. They didn't even look at me as I came in. I was terrified, you can imagine. One of them said 'Strip' over their shoulder and I just stood there not believing it. So she barked 'Strip' again, so I took off a cardigan and my shoes, and then one of them just ripped everything off me and pushed my legs apart and yanked out a Tampax – sorry about this, Linda – and threw it in a bin and dunked me in the bath without even seeing me. Do you know what's worse than being naked and seen by strangers, including men strangers; it's being naked and unseen, because you don't even count as a woman. Why men? In case the women patients are uncontrollable. The bath was dirty. So were the nurses. I asked for a sanitary towel but no one replied. I don't know if they were being cruel: I don't think they thought that what came out of my mouth was words. Well, I was mad, wasn't I? That's why I was there. I was mad because I was a patient, I was wicked because I was a prisoner: they

were sane because they were nurses and good because
they could go home after work.

Linda, is that guy over there in the suit watching? No?
You're sure?

They didn't go far, mind you, most of them. They lived,
breathed, slept The Hospital. Whole families of nurses
live in houses at the side of the great Broadmoor wall.
They intermarry. Complain about one; not complain even
– just go for help, because someone's been tortured,
tormented, mocked – and you find you're talking to the
cousin/aunt/lover/best friend of the complainee. You learn
to shut up: you learn to smile: I was a tea-bag for the
whole of one day and never stopped smiling from dawn
to dusk. That's right, I was a tea-bag. Nurse Kelly put a
wooden frame round my shoulders and hung a piece of
gauze front and back and said 'You be a tea-bag all day'
so I was. How we all laughed. Why did he want me to be
a tea-bag? It was his little joke. They get bored, you see.
They look to the patients for entertainment.

Treatment? Linda, I saw one psychiatrist six times and I
was there three years. The men do better. They have
rehabilitation programmes, ping-pong, carpentry and we
all get videos. Only the men get to choose the video and
they always choose blue films. They have to choose them
to show they're normal sexually, and the women have to
choose not to see them to show the same. You have to be
normal to get out. Sister in the ward fills in the report
cards. She's the one who decides whether or not you're
sane enough to go before the Parole Committee. The
trouble is, she's not so sane herself. She's more institution-
alised than you are.

Eddie, come and join us! How was your game? You
won? Better not do that too often. You don't want to be
seen as an over-achiever. This is Linda, I'm telling her
how we met. At the clinical disco. Shall we do a little

dance, just the pair of us, in the middle of everything and everyone, to celebrate being out? No, you're right, that would be just plain mad. Eddie and I love each other, Linda, we met at the clinical disco, down Broadmoor way. Who knows, the doctor may have been wrong about me not having babies, stranger things happen. My mum ran out on my ex, leaving him to look after the baby: he came to visit me in Broadmoor once and asked me to go back to him, but I wouldn't. Sister put me back for that: a proper woman wants to go back to her husband, even though he's her little sister's father. And after he'd gone I cried. You must never cry in Broadmoor. It means you're depressed; and that's the worst madness of all. The staff all love it in there, and think you're really crazy if you don't. I guess they get kind of offended if you cry. So it's on with the lipstick – that's the first step to a real cure – and smile, smile, smile, though everyone around you is ballooning with Largactyl and barking like the dogs they think they are.

I tell you something, Linda, these places are madhouses, and never, never, plead the balance of your mind is disturbed in court: get a prison sentence and relax, and wait for time to pass and one day you'll be free. But once you're in a secure hospital, you may never get out at all, and they fill the women up with so many tranquillisers, you may never be fit to. The drugs give you brain damage. But I reckon I'm all right; my hands tremble a bit, and my mouth twitches sometimes but it's not too bad. And I'm still *me*, aren't I. Eddie's fine – they don't give men so much, sometimes none at all. Only you never know what's in the tea. But you can't be seen not drinking it because that's paranoia.

Eddie says I should sue the barrister, with his fine talk of therapy and treatment in Broadmoor, but I reckon I won't. Once you've been in you're never safe. They can pop you back inside if you cause any trouble at all, and they're the ones who decide what trouble is. So we keep our mouths shut, and our noses clean, us ex-inmates of Broadmoor.

Are you sure that man's not watching? Is there something wrong with us? Eddie? You're not wearing your ear-ring, are you? Turn your head. No, that's all right. We look just like everyone else? Don't we? Is my lipstick smudged? Christ, I hate wearing it. It makes my eyes look small.

At the clinical disco! They hold them at Broadmoor every month. Lots of the men in there are sex offenders, rapists, mass murderers, torturers, child abusers, flashers. The staff like to see how they're getting on, how they react to the opposite sex, and on the morning of the disco sister turns up and says 'You go, and you and you' and of course you can't say no, no matter how scared you are. Because you're supposed to want to dance. And the male staff gee up the men – 'Hey, look at those titties!' 'Wouldn't you like to look up *that* skirt?' – and stand by looking forward to the trouble, a bit of living porno, better than a blue film any day. And they gee up the women too – 'Wow, there's a handsome hunk of male' – and you have to act interested, because that's normal: if they think you're a lezzie you never get out. So do the men. Eddie and I met at the clinical disco, acting interested. Eddie felt up my titties, and I rubbed myself against him and the staff watched and all of a sudden he said 'Hey, I mean really,' and I said 'Hi,' and he said 'Sorry about this, keep smiling,' and I said 'Ditto, what are you in for?' and he said 'I got a job as a woman teacher. Six little girls framed me. But I love teaching, not little girls. There was just no job for a man,' and I believed him: nobody else ever had. And I told him about my mum and my ex, and he seemed to understand. Didn't you, Eddie! That's love, you see. Love at first sight. You're just on the other person's side, and if you can find someone else like that about you, everything falls into place. We were both out in three months. It didn't matter for once if I wore lipstick, it didn't matter to him he had to watch blue films: you stop thinking that acting sane is driving you mad: you don't have to not cry because you stop wanting to cry: the barking and howling and screeching stops worrying you; I guess when you're in love you're just happy so they have to turn you out; because your being happy shows them up. If you're happy, what does sane or insane mean, what are their lives all about? They can't bear to see it.

Linda, it's been great meeting you. Eddie and I are off home now. I've talked too much. Sorry. When we're our side of our front door I scrub off the make-up and get into jeans and he gets into drag, and we're ourselves, and we just hope no one comes knocking on the door to say, 'Hey that's not normal, back to Broadmoor,' but I reckon love's a talisman. If we hold on to that, we'll be okay.

THE PATH OF RENUNCIATION

♡

Josephine Saxton

Ivor, returning in the evening gloom, told Faith, his landlady, that they had been offered two possibilities at his dull routine job that day. Either they might get a bonus in eight months' time if they worked hard, or there would be a 40 per cent redundancy. It was uncertain.

'So I have formed a new plan. I shall be staying in every evening to save money.' He had been having a phase of heavy drinking.

'Good idea,' said Faith, thinking, well that will make a change, about time he went into another phase. And me too, come to that. Ivor and Faith were both Geminis with Aquarius rising, which to them explained a lot about their apparently inconsistent characters. Faith's ex-husband, who still shared the house until somebody bought it, was a Libra with Pisces ascendant, so that was why he was not so much inconsistent as downright dithery and recalcitrant. Faith's son was away at University, which made at least two people less in the house as he was Gemini also. Her daughter, still at home, was Sagittarius, a very nice girl and apparently the only person in the household not eccentric. That she sweetly remained unaffected by all the lunacy around her proved otherwise. She knew that Ivor was labelled a schizophrenic and had been in mental hospitals, but found nothing odd about him. It was much to her credit that she found hilarious his occasional habit of answering the door while naked, and admired his freshly bleached hair, receding though it was, saying that his new opal ear-ring went very well with the startling colour. Faith's ex-husband, John, had tentatively said that Ivor's hair was bizarre, which was obviously a compliment, unaware of how his own appearance closely resembled that of a Mad Scientist in an early SF movie. He was an academic and his mind was on higher things than his image, or so he said.

'Yes,' announced Ivor portentously as he scrabbled about in the bottom of the fridge for a pork pie which Faith had taken upon herself to throw out because it stank. 'Yes, I shall be reading, and embarking upon a phase of deep meditation.' Joss sticks and loud reverberating Om's from the bathroom, Faith remembered his last deep meditations. But Ivor had told her only last week that he was going out each night in search of a partner for Kundalini sex magic, and she had thought, aren't men all the same, after young girls? She had been peeved because Ivor knew that she too dreamed of a partner for Kundalini sex magic (they both read the same second-hand books from the local Occult Bookstore) – not to mention a partner for sex. Now, because he couldn't afford to go out seeking, he would probably return to her.

She stirred the sauerkraut, adding more peppercorns and sour cream, and announced the imminence of dinner to her daughter by shouting up the back stairs, pitching her voice higher than David Bowie who was making the chandelier tremble. Then she lit a cigarette, poured white wine, generously offering Ivor some, which he declined, being already into his new phase, and waited for people to come and sit down. Ivor too lit a cigarette; both Faith and Ivor had experimented with giving up nicotine but had found it very bad for the soul. John arrived, greeting people benignly. He scattered his bag, coat, boots and a pile of books in various places, to Faith's housewifely annoyance, and took his place at the table, but got up again to feed their seven cats. Their daughter came to the table and Faith began to serve. Faith noticed that the topmost book of the pile was a classic of Tantra. Had it turned him on in any way, she wondered? The book had got Faith very excited about her mystical journey all over again; she had dreamed of the time when she would have a place of her own and be able to entice men into it to assist her in her search for enlightenment. Faith's Kundalini energy was awake and active, but she realised she should put more work into the matter: alchemy just didn't happen, you had to meditate and if possible have ritual sex. Faith had meditated in various schools on and off, mostly off, for twenty-five years. Sometimes she had amazing experiences and made big strides, and sometimes she just forgot about it and became very rational, reading *Scientific American* for pleasure. With the advent of Ivor and the books, though, magic and astral travelling had forced their way back into her existence. It probably had to do with enforced celibacy, of course, but what did that matter? This was a phase full of rich dimensions, why deny it?

Mucking about with powerful natural forces was very dangerous, of course – wasn't Ivor an example of one who had lost his reason in the attempt? – but not so dangerous as simply dying, without having experienced anything rich and strange.

Ivor forgave Faith for throwing out his pork pie – he diced with death on purpose sometimes by eating such rubbish – and prepared himself beans and chips and three fried eggs. That would all change presently, of course: he would embark on a diet of brown rice, raw vegetables and buckwheat doused with a foul Japanese condiment made from rotten soya, full of enzymes. Ivor kept himself awake by giving his body tremendous shocks, and his body withstood these shocks very well, for he used a Bullworker every day and cycled everywhere, very fast. He had been stopped for speeding on his ancient bike, which was very good going indeed.

Faith swam and danced – in phases, of course – and was currently having weekly acupuncture which did amazing things to her energies, rid her of backache and put a grin on her face each time she went. On a spiritual journey the body is the flying car as well as the temple, and must be kept up to scratch. Soon, she must fast and then have a phase of fruit only, for Christmas had been very indulgent and they still felt the effects. Ritual sacrifice, of course, one had to do these things.

Dinner was delicious. Ivor sat next to Faith and she felt currents passing between them. She had been right. He had a bit of a cheek really, because he had neglected her totally for ages and now needed to resume their closer relationship. He used schizophrenia as an excuse for heartlessness: his label could be useful.

After dinner was cleared and the daughter had gone off to play with her two boyfriends, Ivor rolled up one of his astoundingly large joints. They did not always smoke but this was left over from Christmas. Ivor asked John what he thought of the book of Tantra adventures.

'Well, I think the three parts are all beautifully written but very different to one another. I think he is attempting to show the conflict of the two paths, the path of renunciation, and the path of er – the path of . . .'

'The other?' filled in Ivor, causing mirth.

John regained his equilibrium and resumed his explication, passing on the smoke. 'The Kaula episode was rather ambiguous, I thought. It was not, after all, the priestess who initiated him but another young woman – I found it confusing. And of course the Troubadour episode was quite different, as if he had had second thoughts, you know. Courtly love instead of all that futile passion. And the final episode, in the Andes, with the woman dying of TB. That was very morbid.' They watched him as he spoke.

'Morbid?' Ivor was puzzled. Faith interrupted indignantly: 'John, how can you think it morbid, it was beautiful. And he makes it quite clear that the path of renunciation is not for him, not to mention that courtly love did in fact produce orgasm, they used to stand the two lovers in the same room after weeks of tantalising information about the other person, after meditations the meeting of the two bodies produces extreme reactions, you can read about this in my Salvador Dali novel if you doubt my word, the way she will live through him after her death because of the magical ritual is not only a really beautiful description of earthly love, it is all about incorporating the Anima within himself. The book works on several levels, and of course . . .' Here she stopped to take her turn at the smoke.

'Oh.' John smiled at the vase of anemones. 'What I meant was, he dwells overmuch on torture and death and misery and so on. Dwells on it, you know.'

'Three reincarnations, it's three lives, like at the end of *Magister Ludi*. And as I have found, morbid experience is a part of life like the Sufis say, this world is Hell, like the Gnostics. And you can't have light without darkness.'

'Unfortunately,' said Ivor, passing on the joint. They rolled about laughing: it was the way he said things. And then he said: 'Well, I suppose you might think it morbid because the view of the book does away entirely with the present-day domination of the male. Most men don't care for the view of woman as active. Yet it is implicit in Hindu life.'

'It makes no difference to me,' said John equably. Of

course not – he'd chosen the path of renunciation. Or something resembling it very closely. Faith thought, well, it makes a lot of difference to me. Depends on whether I'm feeling shy or not, really. Men got inhibited if you were too forward.

John said he had not found the book totally morbid, he had been most interested at the mention of a group of magicians in Tierra del Fuego, the Selcnam magicians of the Jon people, who know of a city at the South Pole which can only be entered when in an invisible body, the secret of which is known only to them. Like the inverse of Ultima Thule, perhaps?

'Yes, I liked that too. Reminded me of the Don Juan books,' said Faith.

'Made me think of that tab of acid again, I've had it for almost two years now,' said Ivor with his eyes gleaming. 'I wonder if it goes off with keeping? I could do with a trip to the South Pole. Anywhere's better than my bloody job. I hate the boss's son, he's a bastard. I've put a curse on his car yesterday and today his bumper fell off.' Faith was shocked. John seemed not to have heard.

After a while the three separated for the evening, John to watch television, Faith to embroider and Ivor perhaps to meditate? Eventually Faith got ready for bed and settled in where her electric blanket had warmed the single bed she had put in her room. She half expected to hear Ivor tap on the door, and as she waited she watched the shadows of her room, which she loved intimately. There were many hanging plants and a mobile of a hawk made from card which held a tiny plush pheasant in exotic colours. The light came from a huge candle the size of a prize phallus, and the moving shadows enchanted her in her current euphoria. If she flashed the light on and then off, blowing out the candle, stars would glow on her ceiling; she had stuck them there herself, tottering at the top of a stepladder. The constellations were not of the known universe but of some distant galaxy in a parallel reality. One of the constellations resembled a winged serpent.

The room was heavily scented with Aphrodisia incense. Her fluffy and demonic black cat lay curled up on her feet. Her large embroidery of an eclectic Tree of Life winked with numbers of mirrors and sequins. Her books and postcards filled a lot of wallspace, beads hung from a shelf covered in pebbles and semi-precious stones. There was a small poster of a biochemical chart of pathways entitled *Inborn Errors of Metabolism*, which Faith had subtitled *Original Sin Chart*. She loved this room, it was the most harmonious she had ever had. She had restored the pine floor to its original beauty and put down Persian and goatskin rugs. Beautiful. Set and setting were very important – Timothy Leary had been quite correct.

Ivor tapped on the door and entered at her soft permission.

'Hello,' he said, smiling like a Holy Fool.

There did not seem to be an unoccupied chair: each one was full of clothes or books. Faith patted the duvet and Ivor sat near her on the bed, rolling a joint with practised skill.

It was not yet time for fasting and purification: the world was still dark with winter, the flotsam of Christmas still hung around. At such times, expeditions into the underworld are still possible. Fabulous creatures hibernate but if woken with care may lead the seeker to treasure hoards, dazzling miracles beyond the dreams of ordinary sleepers.

The two people smoked in silence. There was no need to suggest or explain. No question of being in love, or an affair, or anything so banal, of course; merely, they shared an electrical current which when the circuit was completed aroused thunder and a roaring dragon power from the centre of the earth. Together, they could fly on a magical serpent which when seen from the ground closely resembled a Persian carpet, a surprising enough phenomenon whether flying or not.

After a while Ivor leaned forward and gently embraced Faith. They kissed dispassionately. Before very long a door in the earth swung open and a distant sound of hissing could be heard, punctuated by a sound like a Chinese gong. Perhaps the cat hissed, perhaps the telephone rang, but at all events Faith began to glow with a haze of blue light and her breathing echoed in her chest with a sound which might have been a deep purr of pleasure or a mantra, *aum, aum, aum.*

'I've got a crick in my back, can I lie on the bed?' asked Ivor.

'Yes.' He placed himself carefully on top of the duvet, a simulacrum for a drawn sword. Faith and Ivor were not playing the game of Quick Screw, Roger the Lodger or Getting Off Rocks, they were following the path of renunciation and the path of the other at one and the same time. Only schizophrenic Geminis can play this particular game in which both win. Together, they silently plotted a theft of fire from Paradise.

So they kissed.

What appeared to happen was that they kissed and touched for about twenty minutes, then parted silently, smiling with complicit bliss. The door gently closed behind a departing Ivor as he went to meditate, leaving Faith with a choice of deep sleep and possible dreams, or certain dreams and then sleep.

The door in the earth was still open and the serpent waited. She extinguished the light and the serpent began to roar, its image glowing in points of light, millions of miles away over her head. Faith was bound to think with a little sigh: I really could use some quite ordinary sex. But it was not available so she began to draw the energy up through the chakras and the wheels began to turn. Now, instead of bliss, Faith's inner vision was opened; she met a visitor from another world. He appeared on a brightly illuminated stage in the form of a very old Jewish man with a curled beard, kindly eyes and a tall hat of black felt which matched his cloak.

'I am the master,' he said. Faith knew by the scent in her nostrils that something was wrong but she glided nearer to him just in case. He flashed open the cloak to show his erect penis and she burst out laughing. Not a Wise Old Man, a Dirty Old Man.

'You're only pretending to be a Kabbalist, really you are a shade from the Qlippoth,' she told him, and he disappeared.

For a long time Faith struggled with garden after garden of earthly delights, steadfastly refusing gratification and beauty in all its many forms, drawing the energy up, higher. Then suddenly she was taken briefly within shouting distance of true and eternal Paradise but, being human, slept.

In the morning she got out of bed a lot quicker than usual. She felt wonderful, no backache, no symptoms of the sniffles which had threatened. Good. Ivor had been at work for an hour but her daughter was in the kitchen finishing off her breakfast, giving the cats porridge from her finger. John came in as the girl left; it was still his vacation. In the bathroom Faith saw that she looked better than for many weeks. Outside, the snow was thick and frozen. That night, they could hope to see an eclipse of the moon. The earth would be directly in between the sun and moon, a conjunction of energies which should certainly be made use of if possible. But Ivor was quixotic and might plead schizophrenia so she might have to work alone. Older women learned wisdom of a kind.

'Good morning,' said John again. 'You are looking very well.' That he noticed her appearance was in itself a miracle.

'Thanks. Eclipse of the moon – it does things to the lymph glands.'

'There is an explanation for everything.'

'True.' The cat which had been ill with flu jumped onto her lap; she gave it some energy and its fur stood up with pleasure. Faith indicated the fresh coffee dripping and asked him if he would like to partake of the fountain of Eternal Youth.

'Thanks, but I think I've had enough.' The cat purred. John took down a dictated shopping-list, the postman arrived and John was perusing something boring. A blackbird perched on a branch by the window.

Faith suddenly said, hardly knowing that she spoke:

'You are Sir Gawain and I am the Loathely Maiden. Tell me, what comes next in the story after she has solved the riddle and they are married?'

'The telephone bill is a bit lower this time,' he said happily.

'Wrong. Go down a ladder,' she said, smiling quietly. She began her wait for the sun to make its shadow in the frozen dark, for then the moon would glow blood red.

DO YOU LOVE ME?

♡

Marge Piercy

Oily night pads in. The city reeks. It is hot, too, in the room under the eaves of the townhouse, where they pitch in bed. He feels all spines. He penetrates her like a question and she responds with her hips, nervously, shallowly.

'I don't know if I love you.' He is sitting on the bed's edge, thinner than ever.

She shivers with sweat. 'Should I leave? Go back to New York?'

'Of course not.' Politely. 'Don't be melodramatic.'

'It's worse since we started sleeping together.'

'Worse?' He shoots to his feet, reaching for his underwear. 'What's worse? It's enough to make anyone nervous, tiptoeing around my parents' house.'

'Why do we stay here, then? Let's go someplace else.'

'You said you liked them.'

'I do. 'Specially your father. He's a dear.'

He snorts, misbuttoning his shirt. Waits for her to help him. In his angular face the grey eyes are set wide. They look past her, anticipating his flight down to the second floor.

Tossing on the cot after he has left, she hears dry voices, the ticking of glib apologies of the men who have borrowed and used her. Her fingers scrape the sheets. She is twenty-one and he is twenty-six, an instructor who was her section man in philosophy, but she is his instructor in bed. She shares herself with him as a winning argument. But he takes her gingerly, and afterward, it is as if sex were something he had stepped in.

At school she had gone out with him from time to time that last winter and spring, times he had taken more seriously than she had. People all said she was pretty; she danced well; there were always men. She had been astonished when he proposed she spend the summer with him in his parents' home. He said they would learn a great deal about each other without being committed to anything, that she would like Boston and find their home comfortable. He was thinking about marriage: that most astonished her. Therefore she did not say No, but Maybe. She took him home with her by way of testing, but learned little except that he settled easily into a placid boredom.

After her last finals she went off to New York, hitchhiking with her one suitcase. Her photographer boyfriend turned out to have a moneyed girlfriend he was living with. She stayed with friends, then other friends, sleeping on lumpy couches. She had imagined being an editor, making the delicate literary decisions she had been taught in school, but she was asked if she could type. She found a job so boring she would sometimes think she would die at her typewriter in the long mornings and longer afternoons. They started to talk at her about dressing differently. She called him in Boston.

Now the house encloses her, like an elbow. The house is as busy with a hundred concealed pursuits and escapes as a forest. His father talks to his mother; his mother talks to the black maid. She and the mother give each other little electric shocks. The father is okay (scotch-and-water, the Maine woods in hunting season, the local *Globe* and the *New York Times*, and a blown wistfulness in his thick face). Coming onto his territory, whether they are to marry, whether he wants to, grows every day bigger and bigger. She rests in his hands like something inert.

He lies in his ivory bedroom. He turns his cheek against his special firm pillow, drifting through his melancholy love for his married cousin Isabel – roses in waxy green paper, Limoges china. Soothing as his mother's hands in childhood fevers.

He feels her in her attic room pressing down on his head. Why did he bring her here? Often he cannot remember. Sometimes she resembles his dreams of the girl who will belong to him, but sometimes she grates. He is amused to think she was born in a Western where names are jokes, the town of Dogleg Bend where dust shimmies in the streets under a sky of mercury.

Once he went there with her, just before finals. Her waitress mother, fat and messy, greeted her without surprise. Her younger sister seized her and they remained closeted for hours. She spoke to no one on the streets. She took him around a maze of overgrown fields and swaybacked houses, playing guide as if there were anything to be seen: that's where we lived the year I was ten. That's where my sister Jeannie and I used to fish on the sandbar. There's where the Massy boys caught me when I was coming from the diner, and when I yelled, they jumped up and down on my stomach. That's where I saw a wounded goose, in fall when they come over.

He has brought her to his family as a well-trained retriever will bring something puzzling to lay at his man's feet and wait, expectant. Do we eat it? Is it good?

By breakfast-time the heat has begun to rise seeping into the shuttered windows. Her face, cool from sleep, across the English marmalade and muffins and yesterday's flowers, seems young again, closed into itself. He wants to touch her.

His hearty father makes a joke about their wan morning faces. His mother suggests with buttery kindness that the girl's dress is somewhat short for the street. All eyes pluck at the seams of bright (too bright?) cotton. Do they know? Their hopeful politeness enwraps him. Yes, they would be glad to spread her on that maid's cot, to serve her up to insure that he is whole and healthy. His mother has always read books on mind-repairing. 'Son, I want you to feel free to bring your friends home.' 'Remember you have nothing to be shy about.' 'I've asked Nancy Bateman – you know, the Batemans' adorable younger daughter? – to dinner Friday . . .' He says, 'Mother, Father, we're going to the cottage for a week. It's too hot here. It's unbearable.'

Her eyes leap from their private shade, but she only takes more jam and teases his father. He knows, in deep thankfulness, that she is pleased and will reward him with an easy day. She will take his wrist in a hard grip and pull him off to play tourists in his own city. All day she will ask nothing. All day she will turn them into magic children from a story. He wants to push away from the table and hurry out with her.

Coming back from the crossroads store with groceries, she looks at him beside her. She cannot imagine marriage. But she knows it is what makes a woman real, weights her to a name and place. That safe feeling she would seek walking in the old cemetery: names and dates neatly grouped in families, even the little babies accounted for. She has wanted to get away as long as she can remember. But being a typist is no better than being a waitress, except that her back and feet hurt less. Bondage.

He says, 'I thought you'd be more struck by the townhouse. We're proud of the wood panelling and the staircase. It dates from 1870.'

But all houses impress her. All other dogs have equally big bones. Walking beside him she catches her breath as they come over a hill out of the scrub oak and the ocean yawns ahead. She is surprised again how tall it is, how much sky it uses up. That blue yawn is her future. She will drown.

The cottage squats on the last dune, facing the sea. She puts down the groceries and sits at the white salt-blistered table. She sits still with concentration. On the table are shells and pebbles she has been collecting.

'I packed my suitcase.'

'I saw you. Why? How can you leave?'

'There's a bus that stops on the highway at four ten, the woman at the crossroads store told me.'

'Why? What do you want to do?'

She lays out the pebbles in circles. 'You don't want me to stay, enough.'

He sees himself returning to the city without her. The air will prickle with questions. Suppose after she leaves, he changes his mind and realizes he wants her? 'Where will you go?' Her paper suitcase stands at the door.

She picks sand from the ribs of a scallop shell. 'New York? Maybe I'll go West.'

Choosing a place so idly makes him dizzy. He sees her blown off like a grasshopper. People cannot just disappear. 'By yourself?'

His tedious jealousy of tedious young men. She smiles. Her heart is chipping at her ribs. Negotiating from a position of apparent strength, she tells herself. The road comes over the last dune fitted to its curved flank in a question mark. She does not dare turn from him to go inside and look at the clock. Will she really have to go?

She concentrates on his bent head: want me! Want me, damn you. She is not sure how much money she has in her purse and wishes she had counted it in the bathroom.

He is staring at his knuckles, big for the thinness of his hands and bone-colored with clenching. 'Do you love me?'

She turns her head. Her gaze strikes into his with a clinking, the stirring of a brittle windchime. He is thinking about girls, the difficulty, the approaching, his shyness, the awful phone calls. She is thinking what she is supposed to say. 'What do you care?'

'I have to know.'

His long milky face, pleading laugh, set of mismatched bones. He is gentle. 'Of course I love you.'

'Do you?' Once again he ducks to stare at his knuckles. She must risk breaking it. She goes to read the clock.

'What time is it?' he calls.

She comes back to answer. 'Five to four. I hope I haven't forgotten anything.'

A strand of hair in the wash basin? Steel hands press on his sholders: decide, decide. His father's voice, rising with the effort to contain his temper. 'Squeeze the trigger, boy, squeeze it. Come on, it won't wait for you all day. *Come on*!' The rabbit bolted then into tall grass. In his relief he shot. His father strode away. Be a man, be a man. Pressure of steel hands.

He has always been fastidious not to give pain. 'Let's walk down to the water.'

She shakes her head. 'Not enough time, I can't miss the bus accidentally, don't you see?' In New York it will be hot. She will call somebody. She will sleep on a couch, and the next day again she will go around to the agencies carrying a pair of borrowed gloves. Men will pester her on the street. Men will buy her supper and expect to lay her as payment. 'I can't sit here any longer waiting for you to decide if you love me – can I?' She claps the sand from her palms, hating herself for having listened to his quiet voice, for having given herself into his hands like a bag of laundry.

He cradles his head, elbowing aside the shells and pebbles. They move him, the sort of treasures a child might hoard. He feels wrong, and is not sure why. He hates the carelessness of men like his father, men in the fraternity of his college years whose act of power was to give pain. He does not know what he wants, only that everything is going off crooked. She is going to walk off with that flimsy suitcase and leave him tangled here.

She reads his face – sullen, puzzled. He will let her go. Her skin crawls. One more defeat. 'Well, want to walk me to the crossroads? It's time.'

But he does not rise. 'Stay.'

Hope scalds her. She wants, wants so badly that surely she must win. 'Why let it drag on?'

'You know it's hard for me to figure out what I feel sometimes. I'm slow to react. I can't just decide like that.'

'You can tell if you love me. You could tell you wanted me here for the summer, before.'

He is afraid, but of what? her leaving? 'But I do love you!' He breaks from his chair, snatches the suitcase from her. 'I do love you. I want us to stay together.' The words slam like a door he is finally through. He feels weak with relief. He has done the right thing. He too will have a wife. He will have a wife and children with his name.

'Then I'll stay.' She stands quite still. That blue future gathers itself in a wave and goes crashing over her. *I've won*! she tells herself. Now I'll be safe. Now I'll belong. And I'll be ever so good to him.

But her spine is water and her hands curl up remembering that vertical house, his parents with their expectant eyes, his ivory bedroom with its air of sickroom. His thin arms fold around her in a tight but formal embrace like an up-ended box.

HERSELF AND HERBERT

♡

Fiona Cooper

Paradise Row lay beside the disused canal, brick worker-housing splattering north from Commercial Road, blocked at the other end by a warehouse wall, high and empty. The two-up, two-down houses had been going for a song at the end of the last war. Mr Whiffen had paid for Number 5 with the lump sum given him after Armistice Day in return for an arm and a leg at Arnhem.

Celia had been conceived in the back bedroom after lights out, although she didn't like to think about it. One grey early morning, the week before her twenty-second birthday, Mr Whiffen had passed away under the sage green candlewick bedcover. Celia's mother had died in the same bed with all the accoutrements of a long illness cluttering her bedside table: a dusty radio with batteries run low, pill bottles plugged with greying cotton wool, a glass clouded with years of soaking dentures, spider-legged spectacles in blue plastic frames.

On what had been Celia's father's bedside table, there was a wedding photo, with her mother clutching the elbow of his uniform, her skirt pleated against her knees in a Stepney wind. That was just before he went on active service, and even after the war, her mother had leant on him and trusted his one good eye to see her right.

After his death, her own eyes had begun to film over and her legs collapsed into trembling waste.

When her mother had taken to her bed, Celia had been seven years into a position at Aldgate East, in a dark brown slice of brick containing Zebrovska's Jewellery Store. Zebrovska had lured the up-and-coming sixteen-year-old with the promise of a move to Hatton Garden just around the corner. As time went by, the prospect receded further and further.

Working days saw Celia with one arm raised at the request stop at the bottom of Paradise Row; on the lower deck along Commercial Road; scurrying across the lights at Aldgate, and the same journey in reverse at six in the evening.

She was sales-assistant, book-keeper, stock-taker, cleaner. The job paid for a series of day nurses while she was out; at week-ends she sat in the back parlour between shopping, reading *Vogue* and *Harper's and Queen*, tense against the hundred or so times her mother would clutch her dead father's crutch and bang the rubbered tip on the ceiling. Tea. Hot milk. Benger's. The po. Read to me, Celia, summat nice from *Woman's Own*, or one of them doctor Mills & Boones, ooh, lovely, they are. And around six on a Saturday: I don't mind if you're out tonight, gel, get out and enjoy yourself. God knows you deserve it, I'll be all right. Here. By myself. And a spasm of coughing throwing her mother forward from the pillows.

For a number of years, she had tried to get her downstairs, in the front parlour, where people might drop in for company. But her mother clung to the wide flat bed in the airless room and whimpered that it wouldn't be right. Up here she felt closer to Him – a blend of Mr Whiffen and her Maker, somewhere above the walnut veneer wardrobe in the alcove. No. It wouldn't be right.

Not to trouble, Celia.

And it wouldn't be right to be lying in bed in the front

parlour, not with the damp breeze lifting from the canal. A sluggish shifting of air that drifted dirt and sickness through an open window, and grimed the glass for all you might clean it every few days.

At thirty, Celia had wanted a change. She sent for a rug on Special Offer in *Vogue*: a Chinese embroidered rug, seven foot by four. More than she could afford, but it was the only thing that was her own in the front parlour, among the ornaments her mother had collected, the medals her father had worn annually, the sepia beakers and silver her grandparents had left them. But the rug was not enough on its own.

At thirty-one, Celia had decided on another change.

The bus took her past the sweat-shops and small businesses whose hand-painted signs went bravely up and stayed over boarded windows: vacancies boards blasted illegible by the rain and the traffic fumes. But there was one sign she had seen through the years that was freshly painted and cleaned: even the lettering re-done every couple of years.

Boondoggle and Company. *Wholesale Imports*. The name fascinated her, and she brightened at the newness of the sign amid the half-hearted decay.

One day she saw a white piece of card in the door, and before she knew what she was doing, she was off the bus at the next stop. She walked back to the sign, clutching handbag and mac against the dirty gusts of air from the lorries thundering by.

The card said: Book-keeper wanted. Apply within. Celia looked at her watch. Once in fifteen years Mr Zebrovska would have to fret the shop open by himself.

For it wasn't right, either, that Celia had seen twenty or more junior sales assistants come fresh from school, as if they were doing the business a favour, and leave Zebrovska's flourishing a discount engagement ring only months later, pinned to the arm of some young man grinning awkwardly, bemused with his bride-to-be and the nuptial rightness of it all.

Celia was as firmly on the shelf as the Coronation tea-caddy in the blistered hole behind the shop where she had lunch, listening for the shop-bell: it's not good for business to close at lunch-time, said Mr Zebrovska, shuffling up the narrow stairs, shaking his head over accounts books that Celia knew were faultless. She tapped on the glass at Boondoggle's.

Heels clacked towards her and the door opened. A tall woman with the brash assurance of twenty blonde years looked at Celia and smiled with a hard orange mouth.

'You come about that then, eh?' she said, waving a gold-banded cigarette at the piece of card.

'I have,' said Celia, standing her ground.

'You better come in,' said the woman, blowing smoke, 'I suppose.'

'You work here, do you?' said Celia.

'Not yet,' said the woman, and sat crossing legs that Celia knew would be better than any testimonial she might wring out of Mr Zebrovska. She was his right hand, he told her, and nobody volunteers for an amputation.

The inner door opened and out came a smell like a West End coffee shop. A good cigar preceded a medium-sized, oldish man in a green velvet frogged jacket.

'Good, good,' he beamed equally at Celia and the blonde, like a fairy-tale gnome.

'Good, come in,' he said to Celia, the smile twinkling conspiratorially away from her.

'I see,' thought Celia. 'The best till last.'

'Boondoggle,' he told her, holding out his hand.

'I'm, er, Miss Whiffen, Celia,' she said, shaking hands awkwardly.

'Coffee?' he said, caressing the word.

'Thank you. That's most kind.'

'And cream?' he said, as if delighted.

Cream was Sundays and Christmasses.

'No, thank you,' she said. 'Just milk, please.'

Boondoggle seemed to enjoy his life: the cups he used were definitely Best – a gold rim around the edge of both cup and saucer. His office, to Celia's mind, was very plush. Velvet curtains and a thick carpet, good furniture polished to a race-horse gloss, a sofa with half a dozen plum velvet cushions scattered on it.

She supposed he was putting her at her ease, but as he rambled warmly about his business, puffing fat little pillows of smoke, she suddenly, badly, needed to spend a penny. What a thing, in the middle of an interview. The po, Celia.

She answered in words of one syllable, heard herself screech with abrupt laughter, and twisted her handkerchief between her hands.

'Ach,' said Boondoggle, gallantly, 'I have to apologise, but I must go and do that which a man can only do alone. You must excuse me.'

Celia's bladder screamed as she heard the thunder of the flush behind the door. She sat grimly as Boondoggle sang a rich and happy song about the sunny side of the street, washed his hands, and ambled back into the room, drying them in the thick strands of a crimson towel.

Boondoggle took her address in a flourishing hand, black ink spurting from a gold nib. He even asked her twice to spell Paradise.

Why bother, thought Celia, her mind going ahead to the long wait for the bus, the way she would have to pacify Mr Zebrovska, and the dank courtyard convenience, where she could never touch the seat.

All that day she wanted to ring Boondoggle: give me another chance, I'm a real sticker, not your flighty type, you won't regret it.

But she didn't ring, and Boondoggle wrote her a note of fulsome regret. The morning she got that, she saw the other woman swagger with blonde arrogance towards the Aladdin's Cave office, with its crystal and silver knick-knacks, its clean windows open to a cool breeze from the river.

Passed over, that's what I am, though Celia, rushing into the teeth of the rain, the sleet and the wind, ahead of the snorting traffic. She took to wrangling with Zebrovska daily over an alarm system, a clean kitchen, a pay-rise, an indoor convenience, the flimsy metal shutters.

'But we're insured, Celia,' he quavered tetchily.

'But what about me? What if some lunatic comes in here with one of them sawn-off shot-guns?'

'No one ever pulls a trigger, Celia. This is England. Now if you'd been in Poland, in 1945 . . .'

'I wasn't,' Celia cut him short. 'I'm in Aldgate East, and this is 1980.'

She collected the stories from the Sundays and the *Standard* about shop assistants plugged with a casual bullet; choked with a cord; multiple stabbings from some desperate thief.

The survey said that eight out of ten violent robberies were committed in small jeweller's shops, and 90 per cent of casualties were women assistants. And 50 per cent of these were fatal.

And Zebrovska did nothing.

The shop windows were the only thing that changed. After the tantalizing glimpse into that other world at Boondoggle's, Celia had started to despise the rows of brown ticketed boxes, the serried ranks of watches and bracelets on the scratched glass shelves.

She had brushed aside Zebrovska's protests of imminent ruin and bought swatches of velvet in every shade. She started to dress the windows with care: royal burgundy or crimson for gold; for silver, jade-green ruched and lavish; for sapphires or diamonds, cerulean blue – even the names were extravagant.

She spent an hour or so of her own time on Mondays arranging the tiny spaces like a treasure-trove, riches scattered as if from a sunken wreck.

'What you need is a nice fellow,' her friend Iris told her in the Crown Prince that Sunday at lunch-time. She didn't particularly like Iris, although she had known her at school. There was something predictably common about her bright pink nails, and the way she drained one Bloody Mary after another; or laughed about leaving yet another job – I've 'ad enough, me! She laughed, too, about her latest overdraft, her rented flat: she was the same age as Celia and had no security at all. Celia sipped a medium-dry sherry, paid her bills as soon as they arrived, and kept up the whole of Number 5, eyes darting around every room for any sign of rising damp, mould, wet rot, or cobwebs. After her mother had died, she did the decorating herself, and was always less than pleased with the way the rooms settled back to what they had been before: her mother and father lingered on, no matter what. Iris's flat was blowsy with pink roses, garish sprays of flowers in her hot apricot bedroom with its wide, soft, suggestive bed, and subdued lighting.

'Iris, don't be daft,' she told her sharply. 'I've done very nicely without and I'm thirty-seven. Bit late, ain't it? And it's a quarter to, I'm off home for my dinner.'

'Never say die, Celia,' said Iris, pulling her mouth to one side in her compact mirror. 'There's a dance in the old girl yet, I'll be bound.'

Iris's laughter followed her into the street. Celia supposed she'd be round later, flourishing some fellow and a bottle of sweet martini, like sin itself. The only thing she could say for Iris was how good she'd been during her mother's years of illness, and all her 'final' turns. She'd always pop round, and when her mother breathed her last, she'd taken all the arrangements out of Celia's hands. For that Celia was truly grateful. But those men couldn't respect her. And Celia thought that respect was the one thing a man could give a woman. Particularly once she reached a certain age.

The Tuesday headline screamed: 'SMASH-AND-GRAB GIANT BLASTS WOMAN.' This had happened in Whitechapel Road. Celia had seen the woman. The paper said she would survive. But in what condition? Celia went cold at the thought of blank years in a chronic ward, wired to machines, wrists tethered to drip-bags. What sort of a life would that be? She blenched when a colossal man came into the shop that morning. SMASH-AND-GRAB GIANT? She looked for a bulge in his coat, and thought of a shoulder holster, like in those American films.

But the worst this one would be, she decided, was a 'palmer' – one of the many who would ask to see a tray of rings and try on several, then slip one into their shirt cuff. As if she wouldn't notice. He certainly asked to see more than one tray, a favourite trick – and then watches, and then bracelets.

'You going to buy something, or what?' she asked him, after twenty minutes or so.

He started a rumble of laughter.

'Truth to tell,' he said, leaning on the counter, 'there was a question I've been wanting to ask.'

'Well?'

'Who does your windows?'

The question was so sincere and admiring that Celia surprised herself, and him, with a warm smile.

'I do them meself,' she said.

'I been walkin' past here for fifteen years, you see,' said the man. 'Me name's Herbert. I never even knew you was here till you started doin' them windows. Makes you want to come in and 'ave somethin'. Beautiful. Like a dragon's hoard.'

Barmy, thought Celia.

'What time do you finish, then?' he said.

'Six o'clock,' she said, and then, sharply, 'why?'

'Well, maybe I could walk you to the bus,' he said, turning scarlet.

'Excuse me,' said Celia, 'I've left the kettle on.'

She whipped into the back room, and snapped the gas off. What was she doing, leaving him alone in the shop?

And when she came back, he was gone. But all the stock was still on the counter. She flattened her hand against her fluttering heart. Good heavens, he could have walked off with the lot. She rattled the trays back under the counter, and spilled a little of her tea, as her heart-rate slowed back to normal.

She opened the varnished doors to the windows, and looked into the little wells of perfect glitter that she had made. They had been noticed, she thought. Funny bloke. I'd never have called a chap that size Herbert. But you can't tell from a baby, she decided.

At six o'clock she locked up, and was five steps out of the door when she saw him, standing there.

'Hello,' he said. 'Can I take you to the bus?'

'I suppose,' she said, and quickened her pace. He stood with her until the bus came, then waved and waved as if she was going on a long journey, and he was her dearest friend. The next day he was outside the shop again, and the next, and for some months the bus stop was as far as he went. Sometimes they had a cup of tea in the café next door.

Herbert had been a cinema projectionist for twenty-odd years and worked most evenings. Apart from that, he was crazy about tropical fish, and entranced her for half an hour or so visiting 'Nautilus Wholesale' – rows of jewel-bright tanks with their vivid plants and scarred rocks, the busy fish nosing the pebbles and darting quirkily here and there.

She often wondered why he'd picked her – he was good company, she found, and must have been good-looking. He always noticed what she was wearing, and Celia found herself looking for new patterns in *Vogue*, and daringly different fabrics; choosing a brooch or a necklace she'd never have bothered with otherwise.

One day he gave her a lumpy parcel, smothered in layers of tissue. She unwrapped it in the steaming November café: it was a piece of coral. She was pleased and puzzled.

'For the windows,' he explained. 'It's from Mauritius. I can change it if you don't think it's right.'

'Oh, it's right,' she said. 'It'll go lovely. Mr Z has got some new abstract pieces in – My idea. It'll be perfect.'

One Sunday she was listening to Iris bemoaning the lack of 'fellows' you'd want to be seen with, when Herbert came into the Crown Prince, and ordered a pint of best in a straight glass. He turned and dipped his mouth into the foam when he saw her. His face spread into a radiant smile.

'Celia!' he said. 'You mind if I sit down?'

Iris arched her eyebrows, crossed her legs, and uncrossed them.

'I better go to the little girl's room. Call of nature,' she announced to the entire room. Celia blushed and wished herself a hundred miles away, or at least the half-mile from here to Paradise Row, where her modest dinner was simmering, and would be ready in thirty-five minutes.

'Well,' he said, 'what luck seeing you here. What a treat. Made my day.'

'Do you come in here often?' she said primly, imagining.

'I only came in here because you said you lived near Paradise Row, and I was hoping I might run into you.'

Well. What could she say to that?

Iris teetered out of the Ladies and plonked herself into her chair again.

'Go on, Celia,' she said through fresh-caked lipstick. 'You're a dark horse, ain't you? Who's your young man?'

'Iris!' Celia blushed. 'This is Herbert.'

'Ooh, Bertie,' flirted Iris. 'Charmed, I'm sure.'

'No,' he said gently, 'Herbert.'

'Well, *Her*bert, when did all this start?'

'Iris!' warned Celia, 'Herbert is a friend of mine.'

But of course, now Iris's mind was on its favourite track; nothing she could say would shift her from it.

By the end of lunchtime, she had gone through every shade from white to red and back again. And, oh my goodness, it was a quarter to three, and her dinner would be ruined. And here was Herbert, and Iris coyly sliding a bottle of Martini into her handbag, and something would have to be done.

But things just happen, as soon as you let go, with a friend like Iris, and Celia's key opened the door to Number 5, and they all went in, the nets next door twitching, as she knew they would, and a smell of charred food filling the house, as she knew it would, and her magazines on the floor with her slippers as she had left them. But Herbert and Iris didn't seem to care, and sat down as she heard herself ask them to, and she fled to the kitchen and yanked the windows open, flung the kettle under the tap and on to the stove, and calmed herself with the routine of making a cup of tea for them all.

She fetched the best china off the shelf and hoped that Iris would keep her embarrassing comments to herself. She washed the dust from the china, and arranged it on a tray, adding two glasses, since she knew Iris, and didn't know Herbert at all, really.

But Herbert smiled a big thank-you for a cup of tea, and laughed gently at the thought of drinking in the afternoon. He talked mainly to Celia, about his job, and didn't take Iris up on any of her many suggestive openings about what might lie between him and Celia.

Thoroughly disgruntled and at the offended stage of being drunk, Iris let herself out at five-thirty. 'Only an hour and a half to opening!'

'She's quite a one, your friend,' said Herbert.

Celia sat and didn't know what to say. He would think she was really like that too, common, and drinking a little too much like some silly old spinster, waiting for men in a pub.

'Now, Celia,' he said, 'I got a question to ask you, and I'd like a straight answer.'

'Well, go ahead,' said Celia, miserably. Why not? What worse things could possibly happen?

'I ain't been walkin' you to the bus for exercise,' he said. 'First time I saw you, I thought you was a woman as I'd like to get to know. I've ruined your dinner, talkin' on in the pub, and I was wonderin' if there was a way I could make it better.'

He was blushing by now. 'Could I take you out for a bite? This evening?'

Celia looked at him.

'I dare say,' she said.

'Well, that's it then,' he said. 'I've been trying to ask

you out properly since I first seen you. I'll pick you up at eight – and don't be late! That's what they say in the films.'

He left, and she stood for a few moments, her back against the front door. Then she went upstairs and opened her wardrobe. There was the dress she'd worn at Margie's wedding two years before. She ironed it, although it didn't need it, and polished the matching shoes, although they'd only been worn once, and opened a new packet of tights. By six-thirty, she was ready, and sipped at the rest of Iris's Martini. By seven-thirty, she had scrubbed her teeth, and sucked several Polos.

At eight o'clock he was there. In a suit and tie, freshly shaved.

From a child, Celia had always wondered about the canal path – where did it go? It stretched along the rusting bridge out of sight, clumps of city-grey grass cracking the asphalt. The canal water was black, its still surface punctured with rusting scummy bike wheels, and jagged iron festooned with tatters of plastic when the water went down a little. She dimly remembered them finding a body there, years ago, but maybe it was something her mother had said, to keep her away from it.

In the summer, small boys stood or sat there, bright pink floats piercing the oily surface, their fishing baskets blocking the path. Down the canal, on the other side of Commercial Road, the canal went by warehouses long empty, cracked filthy glass at the rotting window-frames, GUARD DOG signs askew on rusting nails. Since the fifties there had been no traffic on the canal. Every two years there was a big row in the local paper about who should maintain the lethal spiked fence along Paradise Row: COUNCIL CONTROVERSY! or WATER BOARD SAYS WE WON'T!

When it was the Council, the railings would be some

job lot of lime-green or turquoise, paint splattered as liberally on the ground as on the structure. When it was the Water Board, it would be matte black and fewer drips.

Of recent times, Celia had seen young people in brilliant tapestries of outrageous clothes spilling along from up the path, laughing and talking loud and Hampstead. They would swarm through the railings on to Commercial Road and hail cabs to take their weary explorers' feet back to where they had come from.

She had always wanted to go along the path, and now, with Herbert, she could. You can't go walking on your own at thirty-seven, or any age if you were a woman, it was bad enough on a well-lit street. But Herbert, of course, didn't even have to think about that, and had often walked there, once as far as Camden Town.

They went that way, and the other way down to the Isle of Dogs. These days there was wind-surfing on Limehouse Basin, and they would catch shouts of dismay as the colourful sails dipped, skimmed the water, and went under.

'I'd like to have a go at that,' said Herbert.

'You would,' she said.

'Only I can't swim,' he said. 'Big bloke like me would go straight down.'

She clung to his elbow.

Thirty-eight came with a candle-lit cake with her name on it, and a candle-lit dinner up the West End.

Thirty-nine came too, and Herbert winkled out of her that her favourite stones were amethysts and opals, and sent a friend into the shop to buy her a ring. She enthused over the setting and the stones, imagining the joy of the lucky girl who would slip it on to her third finger: she thought of it fondly, where she had always felt miffed before. Not that she wanted to get married. It surprised her, but she really didn't.

When Herbert gave her the small box, she had forgotten about the ring, but felt a prickle of excitement. Of course, it wouldn't be *just* what she wanted – life never gave you that. But when she saw it there, the ring she had sold the week before, she was speechless. Of course it couldn't be the same one. And she had thought it was an original. Herbert was pleased to tell her that it was.

She had taken to kissing him sometimes, letting him kiss her sometimes. At first she had the idea he was just being polite: that he wanted to was beyond her comprehension. And that she wanted to was a pleasant surprise. And that she wanted more. He stayed later and later. She showed him out more and more unwillingly.

And then he asked her to marry him.

She refused.

'I don't ever want to get married,' she said. 'It wouldn't be right. Not . . . in mum and dad's house . . . I couldn't leave here, you see.'

'I got a place, you know,' he said. 'And I won't stop asking you.'

That night he stayed until past midnight. She didn't ask him to go. The silence grew between them. Finally he shifted in his chair.

'I got to ask you something.' he said.

'Well, go on,' she said, in the shadows.

'Do you . . .' he started.

He left the question hanging between them and moved over to kneel in front of her. He held her face in one hand, and stroked her cheeks, brushed her lips with one finger, caressed her hair. Suddenly she knew that he really wanted her, and that she actually, fiercely, wanted him, whatever that meant. Her mind darted ahead. Her bed was high and narrow – she had had it since she was a child. Her mother's bed? Perish the thought.

And so they made love on her Chinese carpet, in front of the gas fire. In a dream, she fetched sheets, blankets, pillows, and they slept. His body was like an oven and he held her all night long.

He was watching her when she woke, and he smiled.

'You look like Joan Fontaine,' he said.

'I haven't even got my face on,' she protested.

'Celia, you're beautiful,' he said, and started kissing her all over again.

For the first time she rang Zebrovska to say that she was ill. A touch of fever. Mother-naked in the front parlour. Then darted back under the covers with him.

Iris was her usual self at the Crown Prince that Sunday.

'When are you naming the day?' she teased.

Herbert looked at Celia.

Celia thought: Iris, we're honest-to-God living in sin, and we did it eight times this morning on the carpet, and twice against the front door, and I've had to change me skirt.

'Get me a double brandy, love, will you?' she asked Herbert.

'I'll put some Babycham in it,' said Herbert. 'Make you a Wicked Lady.'

Iris looked at Celia and shook her head.

'You don't hide nothing, girl,' she said.

'I don't have nothing to hide,' said Celia.

Celia made living in sin respectable. After six months or so the curtains next door stopped twitching at Herbert's late hours and when they left together in the morning. Iris stopped asking them to name the day, since the day had clearly arrived and was here to stay with no license to make it right.

There were few things which disturbed Herbert's

magnificent calm. But he feared for Celia when she was away from him, having found her so late and so dear.

'I worry,' he told her. 'Anyone could just walk in the shop and . . .'

'Don't I know it?' said Celia.

'You better have a talk with old Zebrovska,' he said.

'Do you think I haven't?' she said grimly, and showed him the yellowing scrapbook of robberies with violence.

Suddenly a plan dropped with crystal perfection into her mind. She looked at it from every angle, then carefully at Herbert.

'What about if we did it ourselves? Rob the store?'

His eyes met hers. By God, she meant it!

'He'd have to put alarms in then,' he said slowly.

'Oh, yes,' she said with relish. 'Let's do it. Thursday afternoon. Half-day closing. Mr Z goes off to the bank at eleven. He's never back before three.'

'I shall have to tie you up, and gag you,' said Herbert, worried. 'Make it look proper.'

'And you'll have to take something, too,' said Celia. 'What do you want?'

Herbert looked at her wonderingly. Then smiled and closed his eyes. He pictured the windows over the years and lovingly described a three-tier sapphire bracelet, a ruby cluster ring, a gold and platinum chain wristwatch. And . . . ah, yes, the diamond drop earrings. Celia added an amethyst and fire-opal necklace, and the diamond-encrusted choker she had draped on royal-blue velvet the day before.

'Why not?' said Herbert.

He came in at 12.55 on the Thursday, just as she was locking up.

'Zebrovska?' he asked.

'Gone,' she said.

He gagged her and tied her wrists and ankles with tender care.

'All right, love?'

She nodded.

He left, and locked the door with his gloved hands, his pockets bulging slightly.

Zebrovska was devastated, and she fussed round him with brandy when he untied her.

'Celia, Celia, my poor Celia, Miss Whiffen . . . how can I ever apologise . . . I should have put those alarms in,' he cried at 3.15 that afternoon.

Celia described a short man with a scarf round his chin, and the jagged mouth of a shotgun. The police visited her at home, called Herbert Mr Whiffen, and took tea, while giving sympathy.

Zebrovska persuaded Celia to stay, on the condition of an alarm button being installed under the counter.

'That'll bring the boys round in a jiffy,' the police sergeant assured her. Poor woman. What a shock.

Three months later, Herbert asked her: 'What about if you come round to my place for tea?' Then, twinkling with delight: 'I've got something to show you. A surprise!'

'Eight years,' she said. 'Eight years I've been wondering when you'd ask. All right.'

Duly next Sunday she presented herself at 14c Mahonia Buildings.

'Come in, come through,' said Herbert.

He had laid a low chestnut table with petits fours and fine china cups with two gold rings at their rim.

'Now,' he said. 'What do you think?'

Herbert's room was light and airy, four floors up. There was one large painting of a spring meadow, a TV and a comfortable suite. The carpet was thick and soft.

'Tredaire,' said Herbert. 'Look behind you.'

Behind her was a huge fishtank, brilliantly lit. A shoal

of kingfisher bright neons swept the length of it. Leopard-spotted fish whiskered around golden gravel at the bottom. Fluid stripes darted in and out of a miniature cave. Inky black mollies nose-dived into the stream of bubbles. Hectic orange sword-tails cruised the upper water, grazing the iridescent green streamers of weed.

Celia gasped.

On the rock, the sapphire bracelet was draped, glittering, and nibbled at by a bee-striped jelly bean with a flickering tail. The diamond choker was half-buried in sand and gravel. The earrings hung in the tapestry of weed, as if a pirate ship had been scuppered and spilled its treasure in some freak tempest. In one of the craggy caves, the ruby cluster ring sparkled like bright drops of blood. The rest of their cache was strewn around the glowing depths, fire-opals deep in a canyon, an elfin sunrise.

'I used to spend all me Saturdays in Woolworths,' said Herbert. 'Just staring at the jewellery counter. I bought me mum a brooch once, on her birthday. It was white metal. I thought it was silver, and I couldn't make up me mind what colour stones to get. So I got the one with all the colours – pink, red, yellow, purple, orange, green, black, and one clear like a diamond. She put it on her best coat and wore it . . . oh, for as long as I can remember.'

Celia smiled and took a cigarette.

It all seemed perfectly right to her.

FRENCH MOVIE

♡

Laurie Colwin

Billy Delielle sat in her study on a rainy afternoon, staring out the window and watching the rain fall in steady sheets. Her papers were spread before her: she was rewriting the third chapter of her dissertation on the economics of the Industrial Revolution, but the rain distracted her. She said to herself: I am not the sort of person who, faced with a lot of work, sits and broods about a husband or a lover or in my case both, and that is what I am doing.

Billy's husband, Grey, an institutional analyst, was away in Switzerland at a banking conference. As to her lover, for two years she had been companioned in a secret love affair by a man named Francis Clemens. He was not quite old enough to be her father and, having prematurely retired from his investment banking firm to write articles and consult to an interesting client or two, he had a great deal of time. It frequently amazed Billy that he seemed to prefer spending as much as possible of it in her company.

Billy was a hardheaded, straightforward person – she was interested in the clearest look at what was in front of her. In the mirror, she saw herself as dispassionately as she saw the rain from her window. She had lank brown hair, blue eyes and no feature that might be called anything more flattering than healthy. Furthermore, she did not one thing to improve herself in any way. She wore no makeup or jewelry of any kind. Makeup made her feel as if she had been encased in glass, and jewelry made her itch. As for clothes, she had long ago realized that clothing was the enemy. It took against her, and rucked or wrinkled or caused its seams to go awry. It dropped its hem which then had to be done up with masking tape – Billy was not much of a hand with a sewing needle. She could not tie the ties on the few nice blouses she had for teaching – Billy taught a class in economic history at the business school. At her very best she only looked presentable.

Of her general aspect, Francis Clemens had remarked: 'It shows how nice you are that you give blind people an opportunity to learn to cut hair by practicing on you, and also thoughtful of you to lend them the nail scissors.'

After two years, he had gotten used to Billy's collection of frayed and shapeless sweaters – most of them castoffs from her husband or younger brother – her faded jeans, her limp skirts and extremely grotty sweatshirts, but he could never stop himself from saying, when be beheld her: 'You really go all out for a guy.'

As she sat at her desk, Billy traced Francis's progress. He had taken his wife, Vera, who was an interior designer, to the airport. Vera was consulting on the building of a library for handicapped citizens in Seattle. By this time, Billy knew, Francis would be on his way back into the city, and soon enough he would find a parking space very near her dwelling. He would bound up the stairs, ring her bell and take her into his arms. Often she could actually feel his arms around her. This caused her to shiver. Her previously safe, ordinary life had been transformed, by the presence of an extraordinary irritant, into something resembling one of those oddly shaped freshwater pearls – Billy knew about these because of an interest not in jewelry but in zoology.

The doorbell rang. Billy started up. The extraordinary irritant had arrived. He hung his dripping raincoat on a hook in the hall and surveyed Billy. This was what Billy called 'mistress appraisal.' Francis looked at her with affection and irritation, and shook his head. She stood before him wearing Grey's worn-out football jersey, a pair of faded corduroy trousers and socks.

'A vision of radiant loveliness,' Francis said.

'I'm so sorry,' Billy said. 'The laundry ruined my filmy peignoir.'

'Get me a towel,' said Francis. 'I'm soaked.'

He followed her upstairs to the bathroom and permitted a towel to be hung around his neck. The bathroom was at the top of the stairs. Next to it was Billy's study where, on Billy's hard, ratty couch, she and Francis had been lovers many times.

Francis was tall and slender. His hair was turning grey on the sides. He looked down at Billy and she looked up at him. In an instant they were in each other's arms and very soon thereafter they found themselves on Billy's couch. Meanwhile, thunder accompanied by dangerous lightning, which brought down a record number of tree branches in Central Park, moved overhead.

Francis and Billy lay on Billy's couch covered by the limp, faded quilt Billy took naps under in the afternoon.

'I'm starving,' said Francis.

'Umm,' said Billy. Love made her sleepy; she had drifted away. Outside, the rain beat down and the thunder was so loud it made the windows rattle.

'Really starving,' Francis said. 'I don't suppose you have so much as a mouldy piece of bread in your so-called pantry.'

'Not so much as,' said Billy, yawning. She was the most elemental of cooks, and Francis could count on the fingers of one hand the meals she had given him. Mostly she offered canned soup, although once, in a rented house in Vermont where they had spent a week when both Vera and Grey were in Europe, she had fixed a plate of toasted cheese.

'Toasted cheese,' said Francis. 'How I long for it.'

Billy closed her eyes. She could see that Vermont house, the plate she had put the toasted cheese on, the shirt of Francis's she had worn into the kitchen, and Francis, looking as he looked now – lovelorn, expectant and ardent, with his hair mussed and a quilt wrapped around his middle.

'Let's go to my house,' Francis said.

'Never,' said Billy, who was phobic about Francis's dwelling.

'It's too rainy to go looking for a restaurant,' Francis said. 'I have some choice edibles at my place.'

'I would rather eat cheese and garlic and live in a windmill,' said Billy.

'Oh, really?' Francis said. 'Where'd you pick that up.'

'It's from *Henry the Fourth*,' Billy said. 'My favorite teacher, Miss Chaffee, used to say it all the time.'

'Cheese and garlic,' Francis said. 'How I long for it. Get dressed. You've given me a ferocious appetite.'

Billy yawned again. She was starving, too. Hunger made Francis restless. In his naked state he prowled around her study. He knew in advance that there was nothing of interest on her desk, so he opened her study closet where her clothes were kept.

'I always hope I'll find something nice-looking in here,' he said.

'Fat chance,' said Billy.

Francis surveyed her clothes. He rummaged in the back

and pulled forth a black dress.

'What's this?' he said. 'This is an actual nice-looking garment.'

'It was at the cleaner's for a year,' Billy said. 'I found the ticket by accident and picked it up the other day.' She turned on her side because she did not want to look at Francis. The sight of him naked and holding up her dress caused her heart to ache. These poignant moments, of which there seemed so many in a love affair, printed themselves indelibly on her consciousness. The result was that even on the happiest day, walking across a field in Maine out on a bird walk with Grey, for instance, these tender spectres – Francis half dressed, Francis grinning, Francis doing some preposterous thing – rose up before her and reminded her that her life was full of thorns.

Francis put on his trousers and socks and sat down next to her on the couch. At his feet were her ratty corduroy trousers. On top of them lay the white cotton underpants he was given to understand she bought at the five and ten cents store. On top of Grey's football jersey, coiled like worms, were two worm-colored socks. The look on Francis's face said: 'What color might these socks once have been? Why are so many of her clothes *worm*-colored?' Billy knew this look very well.

'I'll take you to my house and feed you a beautiful roast beef sandwich with watercress and curried mayonnaise,' Francis said into her hair. She smelled mild and sweet, like a child's biscuit.

'I'm not going to eat the left-overs of your dinner party,' Billy said.

'It wasn't a dinner party,' Francis said into her neck. 'It was family dinner right before Vera left.'

'Eep!' said Billy, pulling away from him. 'How can you utter the word "family" and slobber over me at the same time. Quentin and Aaron are probably coming out in hives right now and don't know why.' Quentin and Aaron were Francis's grown sons.

'Hush,' said Francis.

'You want to feed me *old* food,' Billy said. 'You want to feed me something cooked by your very own wife.'

'Hush,' said Francis again. He put his arms around her.

'You have very long arms,' Billy said. 'Has this been pointed out to you?'

'Many times,' Francis said. 'You have pointed it out on many occasions.' He turned her towards him and kissed her.

'You have the wing span of the California Condor,' Billy said.

'The California Condor is extinct,' Francis murmured.

'It is not,' said Billy. 'It is an endangered species and is making a comeback.' She draped her arms around Francis's neck. Francis began to feel a good deal less like going home to get his roast beef sandwich.

'In fact,' Billy said dreamily, 'the last issue of *Condor Watch* describes how to feed condor hatchlings on simulated vulture regurgitation.'

'Probably very like some of the meals I have had here,' said Francis. He kissed her again and it was clear they were not going anywhere. When they finally went downstairs it had stopped raining and they made a snack of peanut butter and stale water crackers. They were both ravenous and almost anything would have done.

Billy and Francis never stayed together – Billy sent him out into the rain and off to sleep alone in the enormous bed he shared with Vera. She did not like Francis prowling around her bedroom, which he did every chance he got, and she found the look he gave her marriage bed – a rather small bed, in fact – stirred up an enormous cloud of complicated feelings in her.

After Francis left, Billy washed the tea cups, locked the door and checked the windows. Then she went upstairs and got into bed.

The bedroom Billy shared with Grey was the nicest room in the house. Billy and Grey were mostly indifferent to objects, and their idea of home decor had to do with placing inherited possessions here and there. In the bedroom, this inheritance was not only harmonious, it was actually pretty, a fact Billy had seen register on Francis's face.

She and Grey slept in the four-poster bed that had come from Billy's great aunt, and under a quilt that had belonged to Grey's grandmother. Under the bed were hidden the worn parts of the Persian rug Billy's grandmother had left them. The mahogany bureau was a castoff from Grey's parents. Over the sham fireplace was a painting of a woman in a bonnet holding a basket of flowers – this came from Grey's grandfather.

Billy sat up. In the corner was the oak valet that for years had stood by her grandfather's closet. Now it was Grey's, and when he was home his jacket hung on its shoulders, his trousers over its rack and his watch and cufflinks sat in its little tray. When he was not home it was as empty as a skeleton.

Billy had known Grey all her life. Both their fathers had worked in London; and at the same day school favored by American parents, Billy and Grey had met. Billy could easily remember him: a sturdy, wavy-haired boy wearing grey shorts, grey kneesocks and a football jersey. She could see him on the soccer field, his glasses concealing his fierce air of concentration. Both of them had been sent to college in America, and they had re-met when Billy was in graduate school and Grey was starting his career as an institutional analyst on Wall Street.

In matters of the heart, Grey was rather a cave boy. He

had hit Billy over the head, so to speak, and carried her off to his den. It had been their almost immediate intention to marry: they were both the sort who cannot imagine marrying someone they had not known forever.

Thus Billy had been a love object and a marriage object, but she had never, as far as she knew, been the inspiration for anyone's romantic fantasy. This was just as well, since the things associated commonly with romance she found quite beyond her. Perfume made her sneeze. She could never imagine herself wearing lacy underwear – she had worn a fancy slip under her wedding suit and it had bit her, she felt. She did not curl or style her hair, or wear mascara or flirt.

In the known world she was just herself, an economic historian, Grey's wife, a person happier in her brother's hiking shorts and her husband's old tee-shirt. On her husband's side of the bed were his pile of mysteries and astronomy books, and his water jug because he got thirsty at night. Things were in place, had histories, could be dragged out into the light of day to be examined. There was not one secret thing about them.

In the unknown world was Francis, with whom she would never be legitimately connected. She would never walk out in the sunshine with him – not in any place where they might be spotted. The experience of him was undeniably educational in a way Billy had not anticipated. She had had no idea she had all these feelings, but they were not practical. They led nowhere, were not useful and they caused her pain. She rolled over to Grey's side of the bed, put her arms around his pillow, and fell asleep.

The next morning Francis turned up before noon.

'I came for elevenses,' he said.

'Oh, dear,' said Billy. 'There isn't anything for eleven-ses.' A nicer mistress, she had been told, would have kept a little something or other around to feed a person.

'I'll just have you for elevenses,' Francis said. Billy's heart seemed to slip. It never ceased to amaze her that the only thing she had to offer – her badly dressed, sloppily coiffed, undomestic self – was what Francis seemed to want.

'I'm sure you'd rather have a lovely sandwich,' Billy said.

'You'll do quite well,' Francis said. 'After all, I can always have a lovely sandwich. We can have lunch out later.'

Billy was silent. Here eyes were cast down. Francis often said he did not know what she was thinking. This was because Billy did not know. She felt seized, and overcome. Francis grabbed her hand. 'Maybe you don't want *me* for elevenses?' he said.

Billy blushed. She felt she could not speak. 'Come on,' she said. 'Come upstairs with me.'

They went for lunch to one of their haunts – a secdy delicatessen in an out-of-the-way neighborhood which had a sign over the cash register that read: LET US CATER YOUR NEXT AFFAIR.

Billy wolfed down her pastrami sandwich and was watching Francis, a slow eater, slowly eat his matzoh ball soup. She leaned over and took a nip with her spoon.

'Get your own soup,' said Francis.

'I'm much happier with yours,' Billy said. 'Or don't you like to have people eat off your plate?'

'You're the only person who does,' said Francis. 'I like it a lot.'

Billy stared at him. Married all those years and Vera never snagged so much as a chicken wing off his plate?

'Really?' she said. 'Then you won't mind if I take a sip of your iced coffee.'

'Vera feels very strongly about sharing drinks,' Francis said offhandedly.

'Gosh,' said Billy, who knew a cue when she heard one. 'Think how strongly she'd feel about sharing *you*.'

Francis stared into his soup.

'On the other hand,' said Billy, crunching a piece of ice, 'maybe she wouldn't. Maybe she'd be relieved, or maybe she would think of it as another opportunity for good works. Maybe she'd say: Oh, that poorly dressed Billy Delielle. She has so little style in her life. Surely she deserves a crack at Francis to dress her up a little.'

Francis stared even more deeply at his plate. It was Billy's theory that she had been given the function in Francis's life of hating Vera.

Billy was sick of Vera. She was sick of hearing about the library for handicapped citizens which Vera was designing free of charge. A million do-good projects did not compensate for the fact that Vera had strong feelings about sharing drinks.

She felt she knew Vera like the back of her hand. She knew the names of Vera's three closest friends as well as the names of their husbands, children and pets. She knew the history of Vera's career as an interior designer. She had heard three or four times the story of how Vera had packed an entire set of yellow French crockery into her suitcase by seamailing all her clothes home from Paris. She had had replayed conversations between Vera and someone called Dr Holleys Wiener, a director of the soon-to-be-built Rees-DeGroot Library for Handicapped Citizens. These conversations showed that Vera had discovered design angles to help the handicapped that even he, Dr Holleys Wiener, an expert in the field, had never imagined.

She had, of course, met Vera. Soon after Billy and Francis had been introduced at a cocktail party given by one of the financial journals they both wrote for, Francis thought it a jolly idea to invite his new friend, and his new friend's husband, home for dinner. The yellow crockery, Billy recalled, had been much in evidence. Since she had already been told the yellow crockery story at least once, she spent a good deal of the dinner party wondering how Vera had gotten all those plates, cups, saucers and bowls, to say nothing of an oversized platter and a number of serving pieces, into a suitcase.

At that dinner party Vera had been wearing a black dress with bat sleeves, black stockings and black sandals. Around her neck was a necklace of African amber. She was wiry, lean and chic, and wore her chestnut-colored hair piled on top of her head in a stylish knot. She had small, strong, efficient-looking hands, and Billy had already been told a number of times that Vera was an ace cook who had been sent to cooking school in France.

In the dining room, next to the carving knife and fork, and the oversized yellow platter Vera had carried home in her suitcase, Billy had noticed two hatpins one topped with amber and one with coral. She could not imagine what hatpins were doing on a side board, but she found out.

Dinner was glazed duck, and while Francis attended to the wine, Vera prepared to carve. She rolled up her bat sleeves and stuck a hatpin in each one to keep it from unrolling while she sliced. Whenever the thought of Vera kept Billy up at night, she usually appeared in her black dress about to carve the ducks with the hatpins through her sleeves.

And now she was sitting in a crummy delicatessen with Vera's husband, who was reading the paper and checking out the local movies.

'I think we should see *It Oozed from Mars* and *Ghost Dogs from Outer Space*,' Francis said. 'They're playing right around the corner.'

Billy knew that Vera, who liked a film with high social or artistic content, would never go to see any such film. At the same time she felt a stab of something that might have been guilt or longing because *Ghost Dogs from Outer Space* was just the sort of movie Grey liked to see, although Billy would never have told Francis so.

Billy never told Francis anything about Grey. Every now and again he said: 'You never talk about Grey.' If Billy told him something – that Grey knew how to play fives, that Grey had been taught to knit as a child, that Grey knew Russian and read about astronomy – a terrible blank look came over Francis's features and Billy would say: 'You asked.'

She did not know which was worse – the huge bundle of information she was constantly given about Vera, or to get no information at all. Of course, the things they really wanted to know were unaskable.

Billy fell asleep in *Ghost Dogs from Outer Space* but woke up just in time to see the asteroid totally destroy the canine ghost fleet. She was hungry and she said so.

'You have the metabolism of a child,' Francis said. 'You're either hungry or sleepy. In between, you're cranky.'

'Feed me,' said Billy. 'Little children don't have complications in their emotional lives that tire them out.'

'Oh,' said Francis. 'Am I a complication?' He seemed thrilled with the idea.

Just as they had a lunch haunt, so did they have a dinner spot – a Chinese restaurant in which they had never seen another occidental. It was not a very pretty place. It had tile walls, worn linoleum on the floor and the menus were soft with age. On the wall, on shirt cardboards, were the specials of the day, written in

Chinese, although Billy translated them as: LET US CATER YOUR NEXT AFFAIR. No matter what dishes were put before the Chinese, Billy and Francis always had the same meal: flat noodles with meat sauce, steamed broccoli and fried fish. As they began to eat, it began to rain dramatically. The rain was so heavy it was impossible to see across the street.

'Did you ever notice how often we're together in extreme weather?' Francis observed.

It was true. They had kept company during the two worst blizzards in fifty years; through the hottest December on record, the coldest June, the rainiest October, and they had seen snow squalls in April and had once broken up on a day when a tornado watch had been in effect.

'Just think,' Billy said. 'If someone says to you "Remember the ice storm two years ago?" you will be forced to remember that you spent it messing around with me.'

Francis did not say, as he often did: 'I wish you wouldn't use the term "messing around."' He stared out the window and remarked that the rain had abated.

Of course, it was hard to know what other people remembered. Billy remembered each blizzard, each drought, each heat wave by Francis's presence during it. That was the thing about a love affair. It went by frame by frame, unlike ordinary life, which unrolled slowly and surely, whose high moments did not tear your heart apart when you thought of them because they were affixed, as surely as a turquoise in a silver bracelet, in context. The time Billy spent with Francis had a beginning and an end. The middle was full of moments, of one sort or another. It was like a movie – it was like a French movie, Francis said, in which the lovers leave a Chinese restaurant, as they did now, when they thought a rainstorm had let up only to find themselves pressed together in the doorway of an oriental grocery store, penned in by what looked like a monsoon. Billy could see the raindrops on Francis's face, and she would see them many times again, just as she frequently conjured him up naked and prowling around her study, or standing under a ginko tree in autumn and letting the yellow, fan-shaped leaves drift on to his shoulders.

She was half asleep in the car on the way home. Love was full of shadows. Even a baby knew that the man and his wife were stand-ins for the mother and father. She looked over groggily at Francis. He did not remind her of her father. She yawned and squirmed. She longed to be home alone in her rightful bed with her head pressed against Grey's pillow and go to sleep as if she were innocent again and the way before her was straight as a shot arrow.

Grey and Vera were due back the same day – how very convenient of them, Billy said. That morning the sky cleared, and after a week of clouds and rain the sun came out. Francis appeared at Billy's door with a bouquet of flowers in green florist's tissue.

'It's too beautiful to stay indoors,' he said.

'Is "stay indoors" a euphemism for going upstairs and having you throw yourself at me?'

'We're going for a walk,' Francis said. 'In your closet is a blue dress with short sleeves. I'll pay you to take off those repellent trousers and put that dress on.'

Billy went upstairs obediently and changed her clothes. She knew from past experience that Francis had the same sort of feelings Vera had about sharing drinks, about sharing Billy the day his wife was about to return home. These niceties made less difference to Billy, who lived with her conflicted feelings as if they had been a broken leg.

When she got downstairs, Francis was reading her mail – he did this every chance he got.

'The Ross's Gull Society,' he said, holding up a pamphlet. 'A bird seed catalogue. Why don't you ever get any interesting mail? What's this?' He picked up an air letter, clearly from Grey, which Billy plucked from his fingers.

'This is my interesting mail,' she said. 'Let's go.'

They drove to an out-of-the-way park they had discovered quite early in their love affair.

'What an entertainment you are,' said Francis as Billy yawned next to him. Billy could hardly keep her eyes open. In fact, she was exhausted. She had been with Francis every day for a week, and it made her feel as if she had been living in the weird atmosphere of another planet – like a ghost dog from outer space. Gesture, nuance, feeling, poignancy – how draining these things were!

The air in the park was perfectly still. The sun poured down.

'Maybe we should knock it off for a while,' said Billy as they walked to the park gate.

'A first,' Francis said. 'A break-up in nice weather. Do you remember the first time we came here?'

Billy remembered. It had been winter and the park lay under snow. The cardinals, starlings and blue jays called from the bare trees. The great, gnarled mulberry tree had been grey and empty. That June Francis and Billy had taken a sunbath near it and watched two Slavic ladies gathering mulberries into a basket.

Now the park was in its early blossom, blooming with pink and orange azalea. The dogwood and magnolia were out, and the path was scattered with petals. The Scotch broom was covered with little, waxy yellow flowers.

They walked without speaking, each thinking a million things. Real life opened before them: their spouses home in their rightful places. In July and August, the Clemens went to a house in the south of France. In August, Billy and Grey went to Maine.

The next time Billy and Francis came to this park — although they might part for good and never come back — leaves would have turned from green to red and yellow. The cedar waxwings would be eating the last of the crab apples. The light would have turned from gold to silver and the air would be chill.

But now the sunshine warmed them. They walked with their arms entwined. Francis kissed the top of Billy's hair, which was warm and sweet.

A few violets bloomed beneath a birch tree. Francis picked one and stuck it behind Billy's ear. Billy picked a spray of broom and put it through Francis's button hole.

Thus bedecked, they ambled. Actually they were killing time, and putting a spin on their last moments all at once. They might part forever, but it didn't matter. These moments, so vivid and sweet were inalienably theirs — a created thing — as specific and available as a piece of music. They walked in dappled sunlight through a grove of poplar trees, a picture of love or romance in a moment neither would ever have reason to forget.

THE QUILT MAKER

♡

Angela Carter

One theory is, we make our destinies like blind men chucking paint at a wall; we never understand nor even see the marks we leave behind us. But not too much of the grandly accidental abstract expressionist about *my* life, I trust; oh, no. I always try to live on the best possible terms with my unconscious and let my right hand know what my left is doing and, fresh every morning, scrutinize my dreams. Abandon, therefore, or, rather, deconstruct the blind-action painter metaphor; take it apart, formalize it, put it together again, strive for something a touch more hard-edged, intentional, altogether less arty, for I do believe that we all have the right to choose.

In patchwork, a neglected household art — neglected, obviously, because my sex excelled in it — well, there you are; that's the way it's been, isn't it? Not that I've anything against fine art, mind; nevertheless, it took a hundred years for fine artists to catch up with the kind of brilliant abstraction that any ordinary housewife used to be able to put together in only a year, five years, ten years, without making a song and dance about it.

However, in patchwork, an infinitely flexible yet harmonious overall design is kept in the head and worked out in whatever material happens to turn up in the ragbag: party frocks, sackcloth, pieces of wedding dress, of shroud, of bandage, dress shirts, etc. Things that have been worn out or torn, remnants, bits and pieces left over from making blouses. One may appliqué upon one's patchwork birds, fruit and flowers that have been clipped out of glazed chintz left over from covering armchairs or making curtains, and do all manner of things with this and that.

The final design is indeed modified by the availability of materials, but not, necessarily, much.

For the paper patterns from which she snipped out regular rectangles and hexagons of cloth, the thrifty housewife often used up old love letters.

With all patchwork, you must start in the middle and work outward, even in the kind they call 'crazy patchwork', which is made by feather-stitching together arbitrary shapes scissored out at the maker's whim.

Patience is a great quality in the maker of patchwork.

The more I think about it, the more I like this metaphor. You can really make this image work for its living; it synthesizes perfectly both the miscellany of experience and the use we make of it.

Born and bred as I was in the Protestant north working-class tradition, I am also pleased with the metaphor's overtones of thrift and hard work.

Patchwork. Good.

Somewhere along my thirtieth year to heaven – a decade ago now – I was in the Greyhound Bus Station in Houston, Texas, with a man I was then married to. He gave me an American coin of small denomination (he used to carry about all our money for us because he did not trust me with it). Individual compartments in a large vending machine in this bus station contained various cellophane-wrapped sandwiches, biscuits and candy bars. There was a compartment with two peaches in it, rough-cheeked Dixie Reds that looked like Victorian pin-cushions. One peach was big. The other peach was small. I conscientiously selected the smaller peach.

'Why did you do that?' asked the man to whom I was married.

'Somebody else might want the big peach,' I said.

'What's that to you?' he said.

I date my moral deterioration from this point.

No; honestly. Don't you see, from this peach story, how I was brought up? It wasn't – truly it wasn't – that I didn't think I deserved the big peach. Far from it. What it was, was that all my basic training, all my internalized values, told me to leave the big peach there for somebody who wanted it more than I did.

Wanted it; desire, more imperious by far than need. I had the greatest respect for the desires of other people, although, at that time, my own desires remained a mystery to me. Age has not clarified them except in matters of the flesh, in which now I know very well what I want; and that's quite enough of that, thank you. If you're looking for true confessions of that type, take your business to another shop. Thank you.

The point of this story is, if the man who was then my husband hadn't told me I was a fool to take the little peach, then I never would have left him because, in truth, he was, in a manner of speaking, always the little peach to me.

Formerly, I had been a lavish peach-thief, but I learned to take the small one because I had never been punished, as follows:

Canned fruit was a very big deal in my social class when I was a kid and during the Age of Austerity, food-rationing and so on. Sunday teatime; guests; a glass bowl of canned peach slices on the table. Everybody gossiping and milling about and, by the time my mother put the teapot on the table, I had surreptitiously contrived to put away a good third of those peaches, thieving them out of the glass bowl with my crooked forepaw the way a cat catches goldfish. I would have been – shall we say, for the sake of symmetry – ten years old; and chubby.

My mother caught me licking my sticky fingers and laughed and said I'd already had my share and wouldn't get any more, but when she filled the dishes up, I got just as much as anybody else.

I hope you understand, therefore, how, by the time two more decades had rolled away, it was perfectly natural for me to take the little peach; had I not always been loved enough to feel I had some to spare? What a dangerous state of mind I was in, then!

As any fool could have told him, my ex-husband is much happier with his new wife; as for me, there then ensued ten years of grab, grab, grab, didn't there, to make up for lost time.

Until it is like crashing a soft barrier, this collision of my internal calendar, on which dates melt like fudge, with the tender inexorability of time of which I am not, quite, yet, the ruins (although my skin fits less well than it did, my gums recede apace, I crumple like chiffon in the thigh). Forty.

The significance, the real significance, of the age of forty is that you are, along the allotted span, nearer to death than to birth. Along the lifeline I am now past the halfway mark. But, indeed, are we not ever, in some sense, past that halfway mark, because we know when we were born but we do not know . . .

So, having knocked about the four corners of the world awhile, the ex-peach-thief came back to London, to the familiar seclusion of privet hedges and soiled lace curtains in the windows of tall, narrow terraces. Those streets that always seem to be sleeping, the secrecy of perpetual Sunday afternoons; and in the long, brick-walled back gardens, where the little town foxes who subsist on mice and garbage bark at night, there will be the soft pounce, sometimes, of an owl. The city is a thin layer on top of a wilderness that pokes through the paving stones, here and there, in tufts of grass and ragwort. Wood doves with mucky pink bosoms croon in the old trees at the bottom of the garden; we double-bar the door against burglars, but that's nothing new.

Next-door's cherry is coming out again. It's April's quick-change act – one day, bare; the next, dripping its curds of bloom.

One day, once, sometime after the incident with the little peach, when I had put two oceans and a continent between myself and my ex-husband, while I was earning a Sadie Thompsonesque living as a barmaid in the Orient, I found myself, on a free weekend, riding through a flowering grove on the other side of the world with a young man who said: 'Me Butterfly, you Pinkerton.' and, though I denied it hotly at the time, so it proved, except, when I went away, it was for good. I never returned with an American friend, grant me sufficient good taste.

A small, moist, green wind blew the petals of the scattering cherry blossom through the open windows of the stopping train. They brushed his forehead and caught on his eyelashes and shook off onto the slatted wooden seats; we might have been a wedding party, except that we were pelted, not with confetti, but with the imagery of the beauty, the fragility, the fleetingness of the human condition.

'The blossoms always fall,' he said.

'Next year, they'll come again,' I said comfortably; I

121

was a stranger here, I was not attuned to the sensibility, I believed that life was for living and not for regret.

'What's that to me?' he said.

You used to say you would never forget me. That made me feel like the cherry blossom, here today and gone tomorrow; it is not the kind of thing one says to a person with whom one proposes to spend the rest of one's life, after all. And, after all that, for three hundred and fifty-two in each leap year, I never think of you, sometimes. I cast the image into the past, like a fishing line, and up it comes with a gold mask on the hook, a mask with real tears at the ends of its eyes, but tears which are no longer anybody's tears.

Time has drifted over your face.

The cherry tree in next-door's garden is forty feet high, tall as the house, and it has survived many years of neglect. In fact, it has not one but two tricks up its arboreal sleeve; each trick involves three sets of transformations and these it performs regularly as clockwork each year, the first in early, the second in late spring. Thus:

one day, in April, sticks; the day after, flowers; the third day, leaves. Then –

through May and early June, the cherries form and ripen until, one fine day, they are rosy and the birds come, the tree turns into a busy tower of birds admired by a tranced circle of cats below. (We are a neighbourhood rich in cats.) The day after, the tree bears nothing but cherry pits picked perfectly clean by quick, clever beaks, a stone tree.

The cherry is the principal monument of Letty's wild garden. How wonderfully unattended her garden grows all the soft months of the year, from April through September! Dandelions come before the swallow does and languorously blow away in drifts of fuzzy seed. Then up sprouts a long bolster of creeping buttercups. After that, bindweed distributes its white cornets everywhere, it climbs over everything in Letty's garden, it swarms up the concrete post that sustains the clothesline on which the lady who lives in the flat above Letty hangs her underclothes out to dry, by means of a pulley from her upstairs kitchen window. She never goes into the garden. She and Letty have not been on speaking terms for twenty years.

I don't know why Letty and the lady upstairs fell out twenty years ago, when the latter was younger than I, but Letty is already an old woman. Now Letty is almost blind and almost deaf but, all the same, enjoys, I think, the changing colours of this disorder, the kaleidoscope of the seasons variegating the garden that neither she nor her late brother have touched since the war, perhaps for some now forgotten reason, perhaps for no reason.

Letty lives in the basement with her cat.

Correction. Used to live.

Oh, the salty realism with which the Middle Ages put skeletons on gravestones, with the motto: 'As I am now, so ye will be!' The birds will come and peck us bare.

I heard a dreadful wailing coming through the wall in the middle of the night. It could have been either of them, Letty or the lady upstairs, pissed out of their minds, perhaps, letting it all hang out, shrieking and howling, alone, driven demented by the heavy anonymous London silence of the fox-haunted night. I put my ear nervously to the wall to seek the source of the sound. 'Help!' said Letty in the basement. The cow that lives upstairs later claimed she never heard a cheep, tucked up under the eaves in dreamland sleep while I leaned on the doorbell for twenty minutes, seeking to rouse her. Letty went on calling:

'Help!' Then I telephoned the police, who came flashing lights, wailing sirens, and double-parked dramatically, leaping out of the car, leaving the doors swinging; emergency call.

But they were wonderful. Wonderful. (We're not black, any of us, of course.) First, they tried the basement door, but it was bolted on the inside as a precaution against burglars. Then they tried to force the front door, but it wouldn't budge, so they smashed the glass in the front door and unfastened the catch from the inside. But Letty, for fear of burglars, had locked herself securely in her basement bedroom, and her voice floated up the stairs: 'Help!'

So they battered her bedroom door open too, splintering the door jamb, making a terrible mess. The cow upstairs, mind, sleeping sweetly throughout, or so she later claimed. Letty had fallen out of bed, bringing the bedclothes with her, knotting herself up in blankets, in a grey sheet, an old patchwork bedcover lightly streaked at one edge with dried shit, and she hadn't been able to pick herself up again, had lain in a helpless tangle on the floor calling for help until the coppers came and scooped her up and tucked her in and made all cozy. She wasn't surprised to see the police; hadn't she been calling: 'Help'? Hadn't help come?

'How old are you, love?' the coppers said. Deaf as she is, she heard the question, the geriatric's customary trigger.

'Eighty,' she said. Her age is the last thing she has left to be proud of. (See how, with age, one defines oneself by age, as one did in childhood.)

Think of a number. Ten. Double it. Twenty. Add ten again. Thirty. And again. Forty. Double that. Eighty. If you reverse this image, you obtain something like those Russian nests of wooden dolls, in which big babushka contains a middling babushka who contains a small babushka who contains a tiny babushka and so on *ad infinitum*.

But I am further away from the child I was, the child who stole the peaches, than I am from Letty. For one thing, the peach thief was a plump brunette; I am a skinny redhead.

Henna. I have had red hair for twenty years. (When Letty had already passed through middle age.) I first dyed my hair red when I was twenty. I freshly henna'd my hair yesterday.

Henna is a dried herb sold in the form of a scum-green-coloured powder. You pour this powder into a bowl and add boiling water; you mix the powder into a paste using, say, the handle of a wooden spoon. (It is best not to let henna touch metal, or so they say.) This henna paste is no longer greyish, but now a dark and vivid green, as if the hot water had revived the real colour of the living leaf, and it smells deliciously of spinach. You also add the juice of half a lemon; this is supposed to 'fix' the final colour. Then you rub this hot, stiff paste into the roots of your hair.

(However did they first think of it?)

You're supposed to wear rubber gloves for this part of the process, but I can never be bothered to do that, so, for the first few days after I have refreshed my henna, my fingertips are as if heavily nicotine-stained. Once the green mud has been thickly applied to the hair, you wrap it in an impermeable substance – a polythene bag, or kitchen foil – and leave it to cook. For one hour: auburn highlights. For three hours: a sort of vague russet halo round the head. Six hours: red as fire.

Mind you, henna from different *pays d'origine* has different effects – Persian henna, Egyptian henna,

Pakistani henna, all these produce different tones of red, from that brick red usually associated with the idea of henna to a dark, burning, courtesan plum or cockatoo scarlet. I am a connoisseur of henna, by now, 'an unpretentious henna from the southern slope', that kind of thing. I've been every redhead in the book. But people think I am naturally redheaded and even make certain tempestuous allowances for me, as they did for Rita Hayworth, who purchased red hair at the same mythopoeic counter where Marilyn Monroe acquired her fatal fairness. Perhaps I first started dying my hair in order to acquire the privileged irrationality of redheads. Some men say they adore redheads. These men usually have very interesting psychosexual problems and shouldn't be let out without their mothers.

When I combed Letty's hair next morning, to get her ready for the ambulance, I saw the telltale scales of henna'd dandruff lying along her scalp, although her hair itself is now a vague salt and pepper colour and, I hazard, has not been washed since about the time I was making the peach decision in the Houston, Texas, bus station. At that time, I had appropriately fruity – tangerine-coloured – hair in, I recall, a crewcut as brutal as that of Joan of Arc at the stake – such as we daren't risk now, oh, no. Now we need shadows, my vain face and I; I wear my hair down to my shoulders now. At the moment, henna produces a reddish-gold tinge on me. That is because I am going grey.

Because the effect of henna is also modified by the real colour of the hair beneath. This is what it does to white hair:

In Turkey, in a small country town with a line of poplar trees along the horizon and a dirt-floored square, chickens, motorbikes, apricot sellers, and donkeys, a

woman was haggling for those sesame-seed-coated bracelets of bread you can wear on your arm. From the back,
she was small and slender; she was wearing loose, dark-
blue trousers in a peasant print and a scarf wound round
her head, but from beneath this scarf there fell down the
most wonderful long, thick, Rapunzel-like plait of golden
hair. Pure gold; gold as a wedding ring. This single plait
fell almost to her feet and was as thick as my two arms
held together, I waited impatiently to see the face of this
fairy-tale creature.

Stringing her breads on her wrist, she turned; and she
was old.

'What a life,' said Letty, as I combed her hair.

Of Letty's life I know nothing. I know one or two things
about her: how long she has lived in this basement – since
before I was born, how she used to live with an older
brother, who looked after her, an *older* brother. That he,
last November, fell off a bus, what they call a 'platform
accident', fell off the platform of a moving bus when it
slowed for the stop at the bottom of the road and, falling,
irreparably cracked his head on a kerbstone.

Last November, just before the platform accident, her
brother came knocking at our door to see if we could help
him with a light that did not work. The light in their flat
did not work because the cable had rotted away. The
landlord promised to send an electrician but the electrician never came. Letty and her brother used to pay two
pounds fifty pence a week rent. From the landlord's point
of view, this was not an economic rent; it would not
cover his expenses on the house, rates, etc. From the point
of view of Letty and her late brother, this was not an
economic rent, either, because they could not afford it.

Correction: Letty and her brother could not afford it

because he was too proud to allow the household to avail itself of the services of the caring professions, social workers and so on. After her brother died, the caring professions visited Letty *en masse* and now her financial position is easier, her rent is paid for her.

Correction: *was* paid for her.

We know her name is Letty because she was banging about blindly in the dark kitchen as we/he looked at the fuse box and her brother said fretfully: 'Letty, give over!'

What Letty once saw and heard before the fallible senses betrayed her into a world of halftones and muted sounds is unknown to me. What she touched, what moved her, are mysteries to me. She is Atlantis to me. How she earned her living, why she and her brother came here first, all the real bricks and mortar of her life have collapsed into a rubble of forgotten past.

I cannot guess what were or are her desires.

She was softly fretful herself, she said: 'They're not going to take me away, are they?' Well, they won't let her stay here on her own, will they not, now she has proved that she can't be trusted to lie still in her own bed without tumbling out arse over tip in a trap of blankets, incapable of righting herself. After I combed her hair, when I brought her some tea, she asked me to fetch her porcelain teeth from a saucer on the dressing-table, so that she could eat the biscuit. 'Sorry about that,' she said. She asked me who the person standing beside me was; it was my own reflection in the dressing-table mirror, but, all the same, oh, yes, she was in perfectly sound mind, if you stretch the definition of 'sound' only a very little. One must make allowances. One will do so for oneself.

She needed to sit up to drink the tea, I lifted her. She was so frail it was like picking up a wicker basket with nothing inside it; I braced myself for a burden and there was none, she was as light as if her bones were filled with air like the bones of birds. I felt she needed weights, to keep her from floating up to the ceiling following her airy voice. Faint odour of the lion house in the bedroom and it was freezing cold, although, outside, a good deal of April sunshine and the first white flakes of cherry blossom shaking loose from the tight buds.

Letty's cat came and sat on the end of the bed. 'Hello, pussy,' said Letty.

One of those ill-kempt balls of fluff old ladies keep, this cat looks as if he's unravelling, its black fur has rusted and faded at the same time, but some cats are naturals for the caring professions – they will give you mute company long after anyone else has stopped tolerating your babbling, they don't judge, don't give a damn if you wet the bed and, when the eyesight fades, freely offer themselves for the consolation of still sentient fingertips. He kneads the shit-stained quilt with his paws and purrs.

The cow upstairs came down at last and denied all knowledge of last night's rumpus; she claimed she had slept so soundly she didn't hear the doorbell or the forced entry. She must have passed out or something, or else wasn't there at all but out on the town with her man friend. Or, her man friend was here with her *all the time* and she didn't want anybody to know so kept her head down. We see her man friend once or twice a week as he arrives crabwise to her door with the furtiveness of the adulterer. The cow upstairs is fiftyish, as well preserved as if she'd sprayed herself all over with the hair lacquer that keeps her bright brown curls in tight discipline.

No love lost between her and Letty. 'What a health hazard! What a fire hazard!' Letty, downstairs, dreamily hallucinating in the icy basement as the cow upstairs watches me sweep up the broken glass on the hall floor.

'She oughtn't to be left. She ought to be in a home.' The final clincher: 'For her *own good*.'

Letty dreamily apostrophized the cat; they don't let cats into any old people's homes that I know of.

Then the social worker came; and the doctor; and the district nurse; and, out of nowhere, a great-niece, probably summoned by the social worker, a great-niece in her late twenties with a great-great-niece clutching a teddy bear. Letty is pleased to see the great-great-niece, and this child is the first crack that appears in the picture that I'd built up of Letty's secluded, lonely old age. We hadn't realized there were kin; indeed, the great-niece puts us in our place good and proper. 'It's up to family now,' she said, so we curtsy and retreat, and this great-niece is sharp as a tack, busy as a bee, proprietorial yet tender with the old lady. 'Letty, what have you got up to now?' Warding us outsiders off; perhaps she is ashamed of the shit-stained quilt, the plastic bucket of piss beside Letty's bed.

As they were packing Letty's things in an airline bag the great-niece brought, the landlord – by a curious stroke of fate – chose this very day to collect Letty's rent and perked up no end, stroking his well-shaven chin, to hear the cow upstairs go on and on about how Letty could no longer cope, how she endangered property and life on the premises by forcing men to come and break down doors.

What a life.

Then the ambulance came.

Letty is going to spend a few days in hospital.

This street is, as estate agents say, rapidly improving; the lace curtains are coming down, the round paper lampshades going up like white balloons in each front room. The landlord promised the cow upstairs five thousand pounds in her hand to move out after Letty goes, so that he can renovate the house and sell it with vacant possession for a tremendous profit.

We live in hard-nosed times.

The still unravished bride, the cherry tree, takes flowering possession of the wild garden; the ex-peach-thief contemplates the prospect of ripe fruit the birds will eat, not I.

Curious euphemism 'to go', meaning death, to depart on a journey.

Somewhere along another year to heaven, I elicited the following laborious explanation of male sexual response, which is the other side of the moon, the absolute mystery, the one thing I can never know.

'You put it in, which isn't boring. Then you rock backwards and forwards. That can get quite boring. Then you come. That's not boring.'

For 'you', read 'him'.

'You come; or, as, we Japanese say, go.'

Just so. '*Ikimasu*,' to go. The Japanese orgasmic departure renders the English orgasmic arrival, as if the event were reflected in a mirror and the significance of it altogether different – whatever significance it may have, that is. Desire disappears in its fulfilment, which is cold comfort for hot blood and the reason why there is no such thing as a happy ending.

Besides all this, Japanese puts all its verbs at the ends of its sentences, which helps to confuse the foreigner all the more, so it seemed to me they themselves never quite knew what they were saying half the time.

'Everything here is arsy-varsy.'

'No. Where you are is arsy-varsy.'

And never the twain shall meet. He loved to be bored; don't think he was contemptuously dismissive of the element of boredom inherent in sexual activity. He adored and venerated boredom. He said that dogs, for example, were never bored, nor birds, so, obviously, the capacity that distinguished man from the other higher mammals, from the scaled and feathered things, was that of boredom. The more bored one was, the more one expressed one's humanity.

He liked redheads. 'Europeans are so colourful,' he said.

He was a tricky bugger, that one, a Big Peach, all right; face of Gérard Philippe, soul of Nechaev. I grabbed, grabbed and grabbed and, since I did not have much experience in grabbing, often bit off more than I could chew. Exemplary fate of the plump peach-thief; someone refuses to be assimilated. Once a year, when I look at Letty's cherry tree in flower, I put the image to work, I see the petals fall on a face that looked as if it had been hammered out of gold, like the mask of Agamemnon which Schliemann found at Troy.

The mask turns into a shining carp and flips off the hook at the end of the fishing line. The one that got away.

Let me not romanticize you too much. Because what would I do if you *did* resurrect yourself? Came knocking at my door in all your foul, cool chic of designer jeans and leather blouson and your pocket stuffed with G.N.P., arriving somewhat late in the day to make an honest woman of me as you sometimes used to threaten that you might? 'When you're least expecting it . . .' God, I'm forty, now. Forty! I had you marked down for a Demon Lover, what if indeed you popped up out of the grave of the heart bright as a button with an American car purring outside waiting to whisk me away to where the lilies grow on the bottom of the sea? 'I am now married to a house carpenter,' as the girl in the song explained hurriedly. But, all the same, off she went with the lovely cloven-footed one. But I wouldn't. Not I.

And how very inappropriate too, the language of

antique ballads in which to address one who knew best the international language of the jukebox. You'd have one of those Wurlitzer Cadillacs you liked, that you envied G.I.'s for, all ready to humiliate me with; it would be bellowing out quadraphonic sound. The Everly Brothers. Jerry Lee Lewis. Early Presley. ('When I grow up,' you reveried, 'I'm going to Memphis to marry Presley.') You were altogether too much, you pure child of the late twentieth century, you person from the other side of the moon or mirror, and your hypothetical arrival is a catastrophe too terrifying to contemplate, even in the most plangent state of regret for one's youth.

I lead a quiet life in South London. I grind my coffee beans and drink my cup to a spot of early baroque on the radio. I am now married to a house carpenter. Like the culture that created me, I am receding into the past at the rate of knots. Soon I'll need a whole row of footnotes if anybody under thirty-five is going to comprehend the least thing I say.

And yet . . .

Going out into the back garden to pick rosemary to put inside a chicken, the daffodils in the uncut grass, enough blackbirds out to make a pie.

Letty's cat sits on Letty's windowsill. The blinds are drawn; the social worker drew them five days ago before she drove off in her little Fiat to the hospital, following Letty in the ambulance. I call to Letty's cat but he doesn't turn his head. His fluff has turned to spikes, he looks spiny as a horsechestnut husk.

Letty is in hospital supping broth from a spouted cup and, for all my kind heart, of which I am so proud, my empathy and so on, I myself had not given Letty's companion another thought until today, going out to pick rosemary with which to stuff a roast for our greedy dinners.

I called him again. At the third call, he turned his head. His eyes looked as if milk had been poured into them. The garden wall too high to climb since now I am less limber than I was, I chucked half the contents of a guilty tin of cat food over. Come and get it.

Letty's cat never moved, only stared at me with its curtained eyes. And then all the fat, sleek cats from every garden up and down the road twitched their noses and came jumping, leaping, creeping to the unexpected feast and gobbled all down, every crumb, quick as a wink. What a lesson for a giver of charity! At the conclusion of this heartless banquet at which I'd been the thoughtless host, the company of well-cared-for beasts stretched their swollen bellies in the sun and licked themselves, and then, at last, Letty's cat heaved up on its shaky legs and launched itself, plop, on to the grass.

I thought, perhaps he got a belated whiff of cat food and came for his share, too late, all gone. The other cats ignored him. He staggered when he landed but soon righted himself. He took no interest at all in the stains of cat food, though. He managed a few doddering steps among the dandelions. Then I thought he might be going to chew a few stems of medicinal grass; but he did not so much lower his head towards it as let his head drop, as if he had no strength left to lift it. His sides were caved-in under the stiff, voluminous fur. He had not been taking care of himself. He peered vaguely around, swaying.

You could almost have believed, not that he was waiting for the person who always fed him to come and feed him again as usual, but that he was pining for Letty herself.

Then his hind legs began to shudder involuntarily. He so convulsed himself with shuddering that his hind legs jerked off the ground; he danced. He jerked and shuddered, shuddered and jerked, until at last he vomited up a small amount of white liquid. Then he pulled himself to his feet again and lurched back to the windowsill. With a gigantic effort, he dragged himself up.

Later on, somebody jumped over the wall, more sprightly than I, and left a bowl of bread and milk. But the cat ignored that too. Next day, both were still there, untouched.

The day after that, only the bowl of sour sops, and cherry blossom petals drifting across the vacant windowsill.

Small sins of omission remind one of greater sins of omission; at least sins of commission have the excuse of choice, of intention. However.

May. A blowy, bright-blue, bright-green morning; I go out on the front steps with a shifting plastic sack of garbage and what do I see but the social worker's red Fiat putter to a halt next door.

In the hospital they'd henna'd Letty. An octogenarian redhead, my big babushka who contains my forty, my thirty, my twenty, my ten years within her fragile basket of bones, she has returned, not in a humiliating ambulance, but on her own two feet that she sets down more firmly than she did. She has put on a little weight. She has a better colour, not only in her hair but in her cheeks.

The landlord, foiled.

Escorted by the social worker, the district nurse, the home help, the abrasive yet not ungentle niece, Letty is escorted down the unswept, grass-grown basement stairs into her own scarcely used front door that someone with a key has remembered to unbolt from inside for her return. Her new cockatoo crest — whoever henna'd her really understood henna – points this way and that way as she makes sure that nothing in the street has changed, even if she can see only large blocks of light and shadow, hear, not the shrieking blackbirds, but only the twitch of the voices in her ear that shout: 'Carefully does it. Letty.'

'I can manage,' she said tetchily.

The door the policemen battered in closes upon her and her chattering entourage.

The window of the front room of the cow upstairs slams down, bang.

And what am I to make of that? I'd set it up so carefully, an enigmatic structure about evanescence and ageing and the mists of time, shadows lengthening, cherry blossom, forgetting, neglect, regret . . . the sadness, the sadness of it all . . .

But. Letty. Letty came home.

In the corner shop, the cow upstairs, mad as fire: 'They should have certified her'; the five grand the landlord promised her so that he could sell the house with vacant possession has blown away on the May wind that disintegrated the dandelion clocks. In Letty's garden now is the time for fierce yellow buttercups; the cherry blossom is over, no regrets.

I hope she is too old and too far gone to miss the cat.

Fat chance.

I hope she never wonders if the nice young couple next door thought of feeding him.

But she has come home to die at her own apparently ample leisure in the comfort and privacy of her basement; she has exercised, has she not, her right to choose, she has turned all this into crazy patchwork.

Somewhere along my thirtieth year, I left a husband in a bus station in Houston, Texas, a town to which I have never returned, over a quarrel about a peach which, at the time, seemed to sum up the whole question of the rights of individuals within relationships, and, indeed, perhaps it did.

As you can tell from the colourful scraps of oriental brocade and Turkish homespun I have sewn into this bedcover, I then (call me Ishmael) wandered about for a while and sowed (or sewed) a wild oat or two into this useful domestic article, this product of thrift and imagination, with which I hope to cover myself in my old age to keep my brittle bones warm. (How cold it is in Letty's basement.)

But, okay, so I always said the blossom would come back again, but Letty's return from the clean white grave of the geriatric ward is *ridiculous*! And, furthermore, when I went out into the garden to pick a few tulips, there he is, on the other side of the brick wall, lolling voluptuously among the creeping buttercups, fat as butter himself – Letty's been feeding him up.

'I'm pleased to see *you*,' I said.

In a Japanese folk tale it would be the ghost of her cat, rusty and tactile as in life, the poor cat pining itself from death to life again to come to the back door at the sound of her voice. But we are in South London on a spring morning. Lorries fart and splutter along the Wandsworth Road. Capital Radio is braying from an upper window. An old cat, palpable as a second-hand fur coat, drowses among the buttercups.

We know when we were born but – the times of our reprieves are equally random.

Shake it out and look at it again, the flowers, fruit and bright stain of henna, the Russian dolls, the wrinkling chiffon of the flesh, the old songs, the cat, the woman of eighty; the woman of forty, with dyed hair and most of her own teeth, who is *ma semblable, ma soeur*. Who now recedes into the deceptive privacy of a genre picture, a needlewoman, a quilt maker, a middle-aged woman sewing patchwork in a city garden, turning her face vigorously against the rocks and trees of the patient wilderness waiting round us.

A LITTLE BACKGROUND INFORMATION

♡

Aileen La Tourette

'He's so polite,' Mimi sighed as the young man whose name she pretended not to remember faded into a detergent commercial. It was a very old-fashioned commercial, a testimonial from a young housewife with whitewashed teeth. They hadn't changed, those detergent commercials.

'You're right, Mary,' the young man replied in her mind. He always used her full, real name. She appreciated his courtesy, his gallantry.

'You see,' he was explaining, 'some years back they made it illegal to advertise cigarettes on the tele –'

'That would be because of the cancer, dear,' she answered into the face of the woman selling deodorant. The woman smiled patronizingly, and suggested Mimi used the deodorant.

'Old women don't sweat,' she roared, then clapped her hand over her mouth. What would he think of her?

'You must do, Mimi,' Kevin said suavely, from his armchair. 'Otherwise you'd die, you'd suffocate.'

'What's that one called, dear?' she asked her daughter in her most demented whine.

They went off to make tea, and whisper about her mind. At least she was alone with him. He was back after the commercials, but instead of talking about the world as he usually did, he went on about the cigarette commercials. She turned the sound down so she could hear him.

'When they took the cigarette ads off, they had to find new ones.'

'I remember them,' she said dreamily. 'All streams and kisses. Especially the menthol.'

It was a bit naughty of her. She didn't allow him any liberties. He started talking about the world again, just as they came back with the tea, and turned the sound up.

'Thank you, Kevin,' she said as she accepted a cup.

He looked at her with baleful perplexity. They both wondered how senile she really was. So did she.

'Well, I'm turning in,' Kevin said when he'd gulped his. 'Mimi?'

'Not yet. Night and day, much the same thing.'

'If you sit in front of a blank TV screen, I suppose they are. Instead of in the garden.'

'What me to die of exposure, like the Eskimos? It was snowing out there yesterday.'

He shook his head and tramped upstairs. Her daughter followed him, with a resigned 'Good night, Mimi.' Mimi was the cross between Mummy and Mary they had settled on, years ago.

'I wonder what she sees in that blank screen?' she'd overheard Lucy say one night, when they thought she was asleep. She sat, as usual, in her chair in front of the TV.

'Her own reflection. The past,' he said heavily.

Two out of ten, she told him silently. For trying. She never stared at the blank screen, or slept in her armchair. She went to see the young man, in his studio.

'TV studio' was an expression she'd heard all her life. It retained a vague glamour, but very little meaning. Until he invited her to his room, his studio, inside the set. At first she was wary. He might take advantage. But he persisted. And he was so polite.

The studio had a skylight with a bed underneath it,

where they lay and looked up. That was all. And talked, of course. Sometimes he talked about the world, the way he did on TV. The business of the world had gone on over her head, till now. But he brought it all to her, addressing the intelligence she knew he felt in her. She listened intently, with the intelligence. It understood. *She* understood. Her instincts had been more right than wrong, she learned, and she learned why.

'Sometimes I wonder if this is doing you more harm than good,' he once said, after a long talk.

'Why?' she asked, startled.

'Because I'm giving you something it's too late for you to use, and that must cause you pain.'

She concentrated very hard on her answer. There were all those arguments she'd lost because she didn't have the background information she had now. That was all she'd ever needed; a little background information. No one had given it to her, and she had lacked the industry to search for it. Other things had taken precedence. Then John died, and her mind went soon after; and now she was demented, and could think things out.

'Yes, it hurts,' she told him, pressing his hand and staring through the skylight, at the stars. 'But I'd rather have it than not.'

'You're sure, Mary? he asked formally.

'I'm sure, Howard,' she replied. It was so like him, that formality.

After that, something changed. She stayed in the studio for longer and longer periods of time. She was more and more loathe to leave. Kevin and Lucy treated her like a child, and Howard treated her like a very wise woman. She preferred his studio to their crowded little house. They thought she crowded it, she knew.

One day she had an idea. She waited till Kevin and Lucy went to work, till after the old bat next door had looked in on her, all smiles and sign language.

'I'll bet fifty quid she loses control of her functions before I do,' she'd snarled at Lucy when the system of visits was initiated. 'Pees herself all day long. Drools down her sixteen chins.'

Today she smiled and signalled back. Then she went into their bedroom, huffed and puffed and hauled the portable TV outside to the garden. The weather was improving, and she wanted to be a model looney, after all. They might pack her off to a home, and then she'd have to compete for the TV screen.

'This way, we can each have our own. I can keep a low profile,' she chatted to him as she fixed the TV on a folding chair and got another one to sit in. He smiled, opening the studio door, and she spent the most wonderful afternoon with him, with the skylight open.

It was a bit late when they got home. At first they couldn't find her. She woke with a start to find Kevin shaking her roughly. The young man was gone.

'Mimi, what are you doing out here?'

She started to explain how it was better like this, how she'd not be an annoyance. Kevin and Lucy saw the portable TV in the darkness, and she realized something was terribly wrong.

At the home they've found her mostly docile, though unusual. She likes to sit out in all weathers, ever since they've padlocked the TV after ten o'clock at night. Before that she'd get up and sit in front of it, losing her sleep. It's the sort of thing that could affect their reputation.

SOME OF MY BEST FRIENDS

───────────── ♡ ─────────────

Michelene Wandor

don't get me wrong. I have nothing against politicos.
Some of my best friends are politicos. Always have been,
ever since I discovered politics. it's something about their
energy, their pig-headedness, their impossible visions
about making the world a better place as long as you
agree to see it their way. the ones i like the best are the
ones who rabbit on and on about collectivity, about
getting rid of leadership, about giving the power back to
the people, or whatever slogan they happen to have made
up that amounts to the same thing. These are the people
who go on about working collectively in the most
persistent and egomaniacal way, and always somehow
manage to end up in the centre of things, never doing any
actual work, but always talking the loudest and being the
most dynamic. sorry. i didn't mean to go on about
politicos, it's just that once I get going i just go on and on
about it. the other thing is that i'm probably driving you
mad by sometimes having capital letters and sometimes
not. i'm sorry about that, but it's because my left arm is
still in a sling, and sometimes I feel like pressing the shift
button and sometimes i don't. I always do for apostrophes, because there's nothing i hate more than words
without their apostrophes. so this will look a bit like
those long long tracts which all those american 1960s
poets used to write, because they were all so in love with

their typewriters, and instead of 'and' they used to have '&', partly because it was quicker to write, partly because it was technological, and i've just noticed that you have to press the shift button for that as well, so i'll see how i go.

i'm a terrible digresser, a picker up of anything that happens to be floating down the street, bits of paper, people – I'm not fussy, i just like talking, but i better concentrate a bit more – i read somewhere recently that the b vitamins or do i mean the B vitamins have something to do with your concentration, so maybe i need a few more of them.

well. where shall i start? i expect you want to know how i got my arm in a sling. i expect you want to know a bit more about me. the two go together, i think. i just am not quite sure where the best place is to start.

i'll start with Howell. no, I won't. i'll just say a bit more about me – not much, i promise. my name is Tara Black. that's the name i'm known by, though it isnt – im not going to use any upper case any more from now on – my real name. my real name doesnt matter. i decided to call myself tara black after the Avengers – sorry, i boobed – and it took me ages to decide. i thought about honor, after honor blackman, but im not blonde and anyway the name honor is too moral by half. then i thought about diana, after rigg, but if theres one thing i cant stand its all those matriarchal sort of politicos, i mean mothers are perfectly all right in their own way, but ive never been into worshipping anything or anyone and im not too keen on archetypal myths or any of that rubbish either. just things, real things that happen that you know about. and then there was tara king, in the final series of the avengers. now, i think she was the least successful of the three, and i wasnt about to call myself king, that would be like the other side of the matriarchal coin, but i have always liked the sound of tara. its got a sort of fanfare ring to it, and also its something you can just throw off on your way out the door – ta ra, everyone. so its a name that comes and goes just as you want it to, and i like things that are useful. the black was because i always fancied honor blackman, and i just hope no one thinks im being racist about it all. there was a great load of hullabaloo when the festival started about whether i should change my name in case the black women got upset and i didnt dare let on then that black wasnt my real name anyway.

i wont tell you much about my background; ill just say that my life really started about ten years ago, in the middle of the 1970s, when i discovered all these wonderful politicos and they discovered me. until then i had got up in the morning, gone to my office job in the petroleum company, gone home to my little flat, cooked my dinner, gone out to the films with friends, found the occasional lover, never really fell in love, and went home to visit my parents in brighton some weekends. then one evening i went to a film and there were all these women in trousers, and i wore trousers anyway, so it wasnt that, but i realised that the film id come to see was about women who loved one another, and i promise you i didnt know about the word lesbian then, id just got on with it and not known what it was called. now none of my politico friends believed me when i said this to them, oh, they said, but werent people hostile to you, didnt you get flak, werent you for gods sake, oppressed. but i honestly wasnt. ive always been a bit of a loner, and i like men, some of my best friends are men, but i just didnt fancy going to bed with them. until howell, that is. but ill come to that in a minute. but what about our invisible history, they all said, well, i said, after i failed history o level, i didnt think it had much to do with me anyway, so why should who i go to bed with matter. you can imagine that all this didnt go down at all well, but there you go. thats me. anyway, after this film event, i got to know more and more of them, and eventually gave up my job and went to work at the arts centre where the festival was going to take place. just at reception, answering the phone, booking tickets, that sort of thing, nothing creative, just being around sort of thing.

anyway, the festival was already being organised when i started working there, and i was roped in to do dogsbody things, like phoning people up, writing letters, helping to book groups, acts. oh, yes. the festival was a gay arts festival, the sort of thing thats been happening quite regularly over the past few years in london, and the people at the arts centre already had a routine that i fitted into. and that was how i first met howell. hes one of the live wires in the gay arts group, knows lots about lots, is very dynamic, has long wavy blond hair, bright blue eyes, an amazing smile and a wonderfully crooked nose. ive just reread that sentence, and boy, it is like the description of a film star, written by someone besotted. i tell you, it was the strangest thing. when howell first came to the arts centre after i started work there, we were all having a meeting. id sat myself at the end of the room where there werent any people smoking, and the other end of the room was a haze of smoke.

howell came dashing in late – he was always late for everything – apologising, and although nobody noticed it, i could see that the air just cleared around him as he walked in. it was as if he brought with him some sort of aura, that made the air round him clearer and brighter than the air round everyone else. reader, i fancied him. now i didnt know this at the time. it was not a feeling i recognised. i had never had it before, and all i felt was perked up, terrific energy, my heart beating faster. it was quite a different feeling from the one i got when i fancied women. that feeling was warm, magnetic, a little anxious, but secure and comfortable. what i felt when howell walked into the room was insecure, vibrant, sparkling and shivery.

the meeting carried on, and whenever i could i darted looks across the room at howell. i knew he had noticed me, because he is a restless sort of person who looks round at everyone all the time, but i was very careful never to catch his eye. at the end of the meeting someone asked for two central co-ordinators, one for the men and one for the women, and i volunteered and howell volunteered and there we were.

now it took about another month to get the festival under way, but from the minute the meeting ended, howell and i were inseparable. we all went off to the pub to have a drink, and he and i got into a corner and started sorting out paperwork and we got on like a house on fire, as they say. we met for breakfast, before the arts centre opened the following morning, because there was so much to do. at first we just talked work and organisation, right, because that was what we had to do, and we were both obsessive and workaholics, for the first week we worked busily and crazily and wonderfully, organising, liaising, finding the same people pains in the arse to deal with, and the same people co-operative and reliable. howell had a sort of easy charm about him, and at another meeting, he was asked to take on press and publicity, because everyone thought that with his blond hair and blue eyes and direct gaze he would wow any of the media contacts, whatever their sex and whatever their sexual orientation. funny, that phrase. id never heard it until i got involved with all these politicos and i thought it was a bit stupid to say that when you really meant who they fancied, but then i suppose they were trying to legitimise – there it is again, another of those long words – something they felt had been suppressed. you can tell i got quite good at picking up all the terms, but then i was always good at languages at school, mum said.

anyway, howell, with what i now realised was his usual dynamism, did a real blitz on the press and whatever he did, worked. lots of interest got shown – much of it salacious, probably, but what the hell. we had a really successful press conference in which howell was the front liner, and to all the snidey, gay-baiting questions, he made brilliant little throwaway quips, so that he managed to make people laugh while at the same time absolutely showing that he would not be put down. some of the women were really pissed off with him afterwards, because they said he was just using his macho talents to play the camp clown, but i thought he was just great, and if his little act meant that we would get press coverage, what the hell, then some of the other women said i didnt have a political view of it and i said, no, i didnt, i left that to them. because by this time something had already happened.'

that was that howell and i had made love and slept together. not at one and the same time, you understand; the one followed the other as the night follows the day, and this particular night followed the day on which we got the first obscene phone call, and the first letter with abuse printed all over it. the abuse was amazingly comprehensive, and it isnt worth reproducing really, its just enough to say that it lumped together every minority you can imagine, as well as being anti-gay, as if it imagined that this festival was somehow going to take over the world. i must say in a funny sort of way it sounded as terrified as some of my politico friends sounded euphoric about the festivals, all passion and form. well, perhaps thats not very clear.

we reported all the obscenities to the police. i was a bit shocked after the first one, i must say, and it took howell ages to reassure me that whoever it was wouldnt be lying in wait for me. we went off and had a kebab after work and then he could see i was still in a bit of a state so he offered to come home with me. i was grateful, putting off the moment of being alone, and when we got to the house i automatically went to give him a kiss, as we all did to each other, and somehow, and this is absolutely true, the kiss turned into something really quite other. it went on for ages and ages, as if we were both hungry for something we never knew we had wanted. then, breathless, our mouths and faces wet, we stood back from each other, let go and just burst out laughing. i opened the door, he came in, i put the kettle on and when id put the coffee in the cups we sat down on opposite sides of the kitchen table and i said well, this is a how dye do. the best how dye do ive said for a long time, he said. i liked that, i said. me too, says he. were not supposed to, i said. no, he agreed, have you ever done that before, i asked. not with a girl — sorry, woman, he said. no, nor me, i said — i mean, nor me with a man. and that was just a kiss, he said. i looked at him. we both burst out laughing again. thats my overwhelming memory of that evening, us laughing. it didnt seem shocking or surprising, it was strange and unfamiliar for both of us, and because neither of us ever had to think about contraception or anything like that, we didn't, as they say, go all the way, but I will tell you for sure that we both came with great amusement about how different it all was.

in the morning we were both a bit more sober about the whole thing and tried to work out exactly what the hell had happened. were we going straight, for heavens sake, given that we were such good friends even that didnt seem too bad an idea. we were actually more worried about what other people would think than what we thought. we asked one another whether we were in love and since neither of us had ever been in love with a member of the opposite sex, we had no idea how to answer the question. but i must say it had the hallmarks of love and romance – you, know, you walk past someone in a room just on your way to do something perfectly functional like put on the kettle and you cant resist a quick touch of a piece of skin, or you have a sudden impulse to kiss a bit of exposed neck, or bend down and bite a rather nicely rounded bum and then you simply carry on with being functional. we decided, in deference to the feelings of our friends, not to tell anyone about it. anyway, we didnt know what there was to tell.

on the way to work i had a thought. what, i said, if we were simply bi-sexual. you know, sometimes you fancy one sort of person and sometimes you fancy another. oh no, said howell, thats worse than going straight. i mean, that is wanting to have your cake and eat it. a most capitalist and venal thing to do. id have thought you could argue it as most liberating and progressive, i said, and then i saw the look on howells face and added, but then that sounds rather wishy washy and very sixties, and he leaned over and gave me a quick peck behind the ear.

now we didnt know it at the time, but someone must have seen us. we were just round the corner from the office anyway. for that first day we thought we were behaving quite as usual. looking back, i think we were both oblivious to everyone and everything, and im sure people must have noticed. it wasn't till the following morning that i felt we were being avoided. you know how they say everyone loves a lover. well, this was sort of the opposite. we must have been exuding goodwill and happiness, and i swear we said nothing, were careful not to make any obvious little gestures towards one another.

but there you are. people must have noticed. after a few days of avoidance from people, during which, incident- ally, the phone and postal abuse got worse, one of the directors of the arts centre took us both off to lunch, ostensibly to talk about work. but as soon as we got settled in this little italian restaurant, she spoke up. we were throwing a spanner in the works, we were behaving appallingly, we were flirting and generally carrying on like school children and it either had to stop or we would have to leave. what were we, straights or something.

we were quite shocked, i suppose. wed been naive, i think, in assuming either that we could keep things hidden or that somehow there would be no problem. i wont go into the lengthy tos and fros with all the various people over the next few days, arguing that we could no longer be part of the whole thing, that gay meant gay, that bi-sexuality was liberal and just refusing to accept the radicalism of alternative sexuality. we tried very hard; there were meetings at which we explained that we didnt entirely understand it ourselves, that we were experien- cing a new a kind of sexual attraction – new to us, that is – and that we were not abandoning any radical sexual causes. we found ourselves developing an argument for bi-sexuality, which didnt go down at all well with the hardliners, some of whom said we should be sacked forthwith, and not allowed in the building again. well, it was all very shocking, and we clung together even more. once i said to howell that if it hadnt been for all the fuss, we might never have done it more than once and he sort of agreed. it wasnt just that we were being defiant, it was that we felt like outcasts, like people who had to prove that we were serious about what we were doing, and that meant we began to be more blatant about it while everyone else wrangled on about whether or not we should be sacked. we held hands in public, we kissed now and again, and if we did not go out of our way to be obtrusive in showing our affections, we stopped making any effort to hide them while we were at work.

the festival was nearly upon us, and because we were both so important to its co-ordination, the rows about whether to sack us or not went on and on, while we went on working. the very hardline group that thought we should be thrown out – men and women who normally wouldnt have agreed about anything were absolutely united about this – began to get very fed up when they realised we couldnt be got rid of as easily as all that, and some rather awful things started happening. i found dogshit – well, i suppose it was dogshit – on my chair when i arrived in my office. rotten food was left on top of files, both howell and i got a new sort of hate mail, which we just added to the general anti-gay abuse which was still pouring through the post. we still laughed a lot, but there was a tension there underneath, because we could never just get on with our friendship or relationship or affair or love or whatever it was. any sense of romance in the conventional sense went quite soon, and we had to work hard to make a space where we felt relaxed with one another. one sunday we went off for a very long walk in epping forest, which was lovely. we came back to find my bedroom window smashed, a brick in the middle of the room with an obscene message written on it. we couldnt work out who the hell sent it and then thought it didnt matter anyway.

the day before the festival was due to start there was a final checking-up meeting. all the plans for the opening, the press nights, all the organisation was gone over, and then when all the business was finished, there was a silence, a few rustling of papers, and one of the people most hostile to us spoke up. he had two things he wanted to say, the first was to do with the torchlight procession that night, which was to wind round central london, singing and dancing and celebrating. he announced the time of departure. then he paused, and said that he and his group had decided that if howell and i were anywhere near the building during the festival, they would boy- (and girl)-cott all the events. there was a silence. a lot of the events were being run by them, and everyone knew that the festival would collapse without them. i could tell that everyone was waiting for us to say something. i didnt feel angry or hurt, just very very tired. howell and i had been very silent during all the other meetings, i said, since we had been prepared to abide by the majority decision, but since that decision had not yet been arrived at, perhaps they would let us decide ourselves. howell interrupted me. we have to talk about it, he said. yes, i agreed. well talk about it tonight and let everyone know tomorrow morning. the official opening isnt till lunch-time. well all be here, so if we can all get together at twelve, well have decided something by then. you havent got much option about what you decide, said the opposition. howell said wed still like the evening to think about it all, because we would probably want to make a statement. there was a silence and even the opposition didnt seem to want to push the point. the meeting finished, everyone avoiding our eyes again.

once out of the meeting room everyone broke into a frenzy of last-minute preparation. the street theatre group changed into their costumes for the procession and great fun was had by everyone as the rock band tuned up. the floats arrived and somehow there seemed like an excited, united feeling about it all. howell and i joined in, and feeling towards us relaxed a bit from some people as we all got carried away by the knowledge that after all the hard work, it was all going to really happen.

the procession began moving off at about seven in the

evening. lots of people had turned up, there was an accompanying posse of police who were all very good-humoured, and by about eight the last stragglers had left the centre. they were all due to get back somewhere about midnight. howell and i waved the procession off, and then turned round to go back and finalise some last-minute details. we avoided one anothers eyes, knowing that our evening was going to be a lot more soul-searching than any of those people on the procession could imagine.

when we got back into the building it was terribly quiet after the days excitement. howell and i began going over the press arrangements to check that everything would run smoothly. and then i had a thought. howell, i said, i dont think theres anyone else in this building. rubbish, said howell, there are all sorts of people finishing last-minute things off – theres the lighting – no, i said, i bet everyone else has gone.

we went round that building with a toothcomb. no one else was there. you could tell that people still had bits and pieces to do – well, i said, theyll come back and finish later. that procession was obviously too exciting to miss.

we locked the front door, to prevent the idly curious from wandering in, and went back to work. it was a quiet evening and we worked with hardly a word. by about ten o clock we had finished and the moment could not be put off any longer. well, said howell. well, i said, i dont want to make any statement. i just want to go home and never come back. good, said howell, so do i. ive never really been a politico, i said, well, not like some of the others think they are. howell said, oh, i dont know. theres different ways of being political. anyway, i said, thats what i want to do. and theres another thing. i know, said howell. yes, i said, i know you know. howell said it for me: that we shouldnt see each other for a little while, until after the festival perhaps, and then we could see what we both felt. well, i said, if were both thinking the same sort of thing, it must be a good sign. we looked at each other. then, without saying anything, we went into the theatre and made love on the stage, in the middle of a jumble of a set, using the cushions that were there, adjusting soft lighting and putting on a billie holliday record. we lay there for a little while, still very quiet, then i got up and got dressed and went off to have a pee. i put a kettle on and made some coffee, put it on a tray with some biscuits and went back into the theatre.

just as i pushed the swing doors open, the explosion happened. i was thrown backwards, out of the theatre and my left arm got caught in the doors.

the hospital did a marvellous job with my arm. they actually sewed it back on – after, that is, they had found it, thrown on the other side of the theatre. there was nothing they could do for howell.

i was in hospital for a while. the inquest and funeral all happened while i was still in hospital, and i cried. i had lots of visitors, with much sympathy and support. the police investigated, but could not find any sure source for the people who had planted the bomb. some of the politicos were annoyed because they felt the police hadnt tried hard enough, and had just dismissed it as one loony gesture towards a lot of other loony people. i dont know about that. that may be the right way to look at it. quite frankly, i didnt care whether they found out or not. it wouldnt bring howell back; it wouldnt change anything important.

when i came out of hospital there was a memorial meeting arranged for howell, at the arts centre. i went. some people avoided me completely, a few others – the ones whod come to see me in hospital – were friendly, as usual, and full of excited chat about the festival the following year. the arts centre would be rebuilt and the insurance was going to pay for the new lighting board they always wanted. i had a momentary impulse to ask if there was a job going, but because i knew it was an ironic impulse, i didnt say anything, just said ta-ra as i left the building.

after the meeting i left london and came back to brighton. my left arm is still in a sling, although it isnt like that all the time. its just that i have to rest it as well as move it, if you follow me. i think of howell very often. i wonder whether he was a martyr, willing or unwilling; hes been taken up by lots of his friends as a martyr, and thats fair enough for them. perhaps if howell had been in their shoes he would have felt the same. anyway. last night i met a woman i liked a lot. i fancied her, even. shes married, has a daughter and seems perfectly happy as she is. but there was something in her eyes when she looked at me. ill always recognise that sort of look. its exactly the same look howell had in his eyes at that first meeting.

some of my best friends are still politicos.

JUNK MAIL

♡

Rebecca Brown

I get all this junk in the mail. It bothers me. The audacity of anyone to think they have the right to cram their shit into my mail box. I throw it away.

On the other hand, it is about the only thing I ever get. I mean, other than bills, the odd postcard from people I know on fascinating vacations, late Christmas cards, letters from my aunt in Wichita Falls. Letters I would forward to you if I knew where you were: 'No Longer at This Address.' Not much, in other words, worth writing home about.

So I toss it into the pile that continues to grow, daily, by my desk. Someday, I'm going to throw it all out together, or make a bonfire, something severe and beautiful. Meanwhile, it gets to be a mess.

I hate the thought of it. Obviously everyone in my apartment is subject to the same invasion. People all over town, all over the country, the world. Just think of the waste – the paper, the person-hours, the effort the postal people go through toting it around. Think of their blisters and sunburn, their aching shoulders. Think of the money stores pay those damned fools to design and package and disseminate this shit that no-one wants to buy, that no-one even wants to know about.

I think of warehouses upon warehouses, acres of the same Pay 'N Save booklets with detachable coupons, the billions of Safeway fliers advertising pot-roast specials through Friday, the special trial offers from *New Times*, the Christmas in July sales at Fred's Easy Mart, the slick magazine formats from god-knows-where with three-color printing of bronzed baby shoes and plates with the Presidents' faces. I think of how much more room there'd be in the world without it. I think of fields and open air, a different and more easy kind of room.

It's not just the excess that makes it bad, but excess without reason. The bottom line, what it all boils down to, is: *I don't want this shit.*

Have they ever asked? Do they think I'll believe their impossible promises, their idle threats: You May Already Be a Winner, Order by Midnight Tonight?

But I wondered.

I began to glance at them. Gradually at first. Never more than one per batch, and only the interesting looking ones. I started opening some of the glossy ones with the really with-it graphics, the fat ones that felt like they contained a free sample inside. I'd open these clandestinely, tossing the rest of them into the ever widening pile by my desk. I'd feel almost furtive, until I remind myself that my interest in this was purely academic, research so that I would know exactly what to say when I finally got around to writing the huffy, indignant, and scathingly articulate letters to the Boards of Directors of these companies that plagued me, when I finally told them, with great finesse and sharp and righteous wrath, that my mail box is not just anybody's, into which they and their sleazy little bulk mailing morons could ram anything they felt like, yours sincerely, etc., etc., etc.

I imagined the guy on the other end of my very pointed and very personal epistle: a fat cat, the Chairman of the Board, a big beefy guy in a pin-striped suit, his college tie loosened, his sleeves rolled up, him chewing a soggy cigar and juggling fourteen conference calls from New York, L.A. and London all at once. He's standing at the window in his fiftieth-floor executive suite in Chicago, looking out over the dim gray cityscape, his back to me. I see the back of his head, his bullish neck. Will he read his important private mail? Will he read my desperate message? I think he must. I see him sigh, his heavy shoulders rise and fall. I think he will. I see him turn, his thin and graceful neck. I think he already has. I see his cheeks, so high and fine. I think he has. I see his collar's loose, like yours. He has. I think he's you. He is.

So.

I know why I'm getting all this junk. It's you – sending me a secret message, the only way you think you can get to me through all that is surrounding you, what you've built up.

Darling, why don't you just give me a call?

I look through all of it. I search your secret message in the fine print underneath the unbelievable offers, the 150 valuable coupons, Sizzling Summer Savings, and Dollar Day brochures. There's nothing I can recognize of you right off. On the other hand, what if I really am a winner already? What if I order by midnight tonight? You want me to know this, don't you?

But I won't get distracted. It could be a trick. It could be you wanting to see if I'll turn my head as easily as you always used to say I did – I never did – if I'll let my attention from you lag. Though I have never, ever, forgotten what we're up to, our true purpose here.

I know that there's a message in the junk mail that you

send to me, a secret clue of what you want from me, a hint of how to find you. The catchy leaflets telling me about factory close-outs, final liquidations, about going-out-of-business sales, mean something clear about us.

But you never will go out of business, will you? It's just a new variation on your silly old offer-good-for-a-limited-time-only line, your standard order-by-midnight-tonight ploy. I've called. You know I've called. But your operators aren't standing by your toll free number to take my call. What do you want from me? I've tried to dial you direct.

My last resort, and what I've always feared:
To Whom It May Concern:

It has come to my attention that I am still on your mailing list. I have tried, repeatedly, to be removed, but I keep getting this junk from you. Not even junk, just promises of junk. Shady offers, Computer-generated responses: 'Dear Customer, Thank you for your continued interest in our product line . . .' Don't you read my letters? Don't you understand? My mail box is mine. You've followed me through three changes of address. I don't know where you are. How do you find me? I don't want to be on your mailing list. My mail box is not just anybody's into which you can ram . . .

Yours truly, etc., etc., etc.

But it still comes. Just today – an offer to subscribe to a new long-distance phone-call system, the Sears Vacation Wear Catalogue for People on the Go, 25 per cent off on a pair of season tickets for a theater we only went to once.

How can I express to you how desperately I want to be left alone, to be free of your recycled goods cluttering up my mail box, my desk, my house? I don't give the P.O. my change of address card, but you're so clever you keep finding me.

I know what I'm going to do. I'm going to play your own trick back on you. I'm going to send it all back to you. Though nothing you have ever sent me has included your return address. I'm going to find you. On your own turf, wherever that is, the space you said you needed.

See, here I am, walking to the P.O. Can you hear me? I'm sliding gracefully into the blue tall shiny 'out of town' box, resting sweetly against the soft flat backs of a hundred sleepy travellers like me.

I imagine myself a bird. I imagine myself in the belly of a plane, jostling with the other packages and letters, calm sweet letters from moms to kids, tense letters from overseas lawyers. I imagine sleeping next to a dewy-eyed love letter, breathing in the perfumed scent of love.

I'll slip in through the gorgeous slim mail slot in your exquisite new apartment. I'm thin and lithe and cool and dry and sharp.

But of course I'm only dreaming that. As if I could fit into an envelope.

No, I'm afraid the only way that I'll get back to you will be hard. I'll wrap myself in styrofoam peanuts, tape shut my mouth and eyes, my waiting body. I'll send me back to you, my love. I'm coming back to you.

It isn't just an ordinary box I'm in, but I don't notice this until I wake up in your tender arms again.

It's dark in here. I feel your smooth hands on my back. I'm curled inside this tiny box, tiny and crunched and bent, and you're winding me up, turning a crank behind me and above me, in my back. And every crank you turn gets me wound tighter, waiting, busting to spring. My skin tightens, about to pop. I feel my lips pull back. This box is metal, not the soft, light, giving brown cardboard

I'd crawled inside at the P.O., but tin, painted with garish pictures on the outside, of carousels, balloons, and clowns with big red noses. I'm inside this little box and that crank is cranking into me tighter and tighter, tearing through my bright red and yellow and blue and green checked nylon top, my fuzzy orange wig with the silly exaggerated bald spot, my goofy bright red lips, the two bright cheery dots of pink, my cheeks. And you're still winding me tighter and tighter, and every twist you turn gets me more tense. I'm tighter, harder, smaller. My neck is arcing back into my chest. My bent arms squash into my ribs. My knees crush up against my sides. My face twists. I'm trying to scream, 'Just spring me out, goddammit, let me go!' but my neck is crushed and I can hardly breathe.

Above me, echoing against the tin-bronze colored roof, I hear your voice saying words that I can't understand. A chipper little circus tune tinkles along as you crank.

When the crank is wound so tight that even you can't crank it any more, when I'm so tight and doubled over, about to burst, that's when we both breathe a breath that's quiet, just alike. We hold it, then – pop! – I spew out from the lid, my arms shot apart like unconnected sleeves, little red bits of my fingers splattered like pimentos on the ceiling, my ribs cracked sideways, my torso gouged, my face split like a curtain.

This is too much even for you. You realize, truly and at last, that you don't want this. You truly want to send me back. But who will you send me to now?

So I start getting real things in the mail. Not just the idle offers that I have been.

Boxes start arriving. I'm eager to unwrap them. I do it quickly. You've wrapped them carefully, almost lovingly. First in a plastic wrap, and then in tissue paper, padded with newsprint and styrofoam peanuts, all that inside a box, then wrapped around with P.O. approved paper and string. I think of you wrapping them so carefully, and me unwrapping them, on my side, tenderly.

But, careful as you are, the packages get tossed around, and the fragile soft insides come soaking through. I stumble to my mail box each day in hope that you've sent me back more.

These packages contain: my hands, the soft part of my thigh, that wet red muscle deep inside my chest, etc.

Obviously, it can't last forever.

But somehow, even after you've sent back all that I thought you got of me, there's more. Where do you get this extra stuff? And how do I keep finding room for it all?

I imagine my whole apartment, my entire building, packed to the ceiling with these soggy boxes. Don't you realize I've had enough? Don't you know I don't want this any more? Don't you understand? The P.O. will refuse to deliver all these red soaked packages. You can't keep this up forever.

But I can't rely on the P.O. to stop. They must be in with you. They'll find me out, and follow me. And I believe, I truly believe, that neither rain, nor sleet, nor snow, etc., etc., etc., will stop them or stop you.

There's just one way to get away. Further away than the Pony Express. Further away than anything: an island.

So I see this island.

I see myself. I'm floating above it like a silent, separate eye, hovering, without form or body, hanging in the sky above a tropical paradise. It's a tiny island from above, not more than a couple of miles across. It's mostly sand – harsh, brittle, bright – a hard little nut of white in the perfect sea. I see jagged little shapes where the sand juts into the deep blue, dark green sea. There are lagoons of still dark water. The water is still. The island is mostly sand, but there are groups of palm trees and coconut trees, some places that must be shady. And there must be caves, cool places hidden from the sun. And maybe there's a little hut I've tried to sling together from palm branches and driftwood. And maybe there's a soft place on the ground I've cleared away beneath a tree where I can rest. Because I'm on the island. Yes, that's me. I'm the little small shape I see below me, so tiny and sharp. I watch all my little movements, and from this height, even if in fact they're smooth and calm, they all look tiny and fast, nervous and twitchy as a rodent. I can't tell what I'm trying to do from this height. I think perhaps I'm only trying to rest.

But it's so hard to tell from here. I don't want to leave this distant, cool blue sky, but as soon as I wonder too much what's going on down there, I get pulled down.

So here I am. I'm on the island now and it's hot. It's really hot.

My bare feet are hot in the sand. I'm not sure how big this place is, but I know I'll survive. At least, though I'm still panting from my rough arrival here, I know that somehow, finally, I'll be allowed to breathe easier, both my heaving lungs intact. I'm still wet and my skin still burns.

It wasn't easy getting here. It's the furthest point from anywhere.

The water is deep and blue, dark green. It's still and smooth, not choppy.

I don't know what I'll eat. I've no idea what the seasons are. I look down at the bright white sand between my feet. I close my eyes. I imagine this island covered with white, the tops of palm trees poking out, their big leaves sagging under the coat of fine white powder. I imagine myself the Little Match Girl, standing on the street corner, trying to sell pencils in it. No – no – I squint my eyes tighter and clench my teeth until I imagine myself skiing and graceful, my calves firm, my back strong, down taut monstrous alps of it. I feel cold spray on my face as I whup the ski poles beside me with my confident, sure hands. My throat feels cool. But when I start to swallow, I choke.

I snap my eyes open and blink. I slap my cheeks. I'm hot, really hot. There's sweat on my eyes. I stretch up slowly, an effort, and walk the few steps to the beach, dip my hands into the water and bring it to my face and splash. I look down at the water. It's wavy. I know there's shade somewhere on this island, I've just got to find it. I cup my hands into the water again and bring them to my mouth and drink. I squat by the water and look for signs of fish or mussels or something green and living. But the water is perfectly clear. My stomach growls. I dip my hands in again, press them flat, fingers spread against the soft floor of the water. My wrists make pretty rings, circles in the water. I watch the circles circle out into the smooth, clear, flat lagoon. Across the lagoon from me, a hundred yards to my left, I see the water in the rings suck down, the valleys of waves, then roll up again and crash, huge now, against both sides of the lagoon I'm at the apex of. I pull my hands out of the water and squat further back on the ground, my innocent hands limp at my sides. I look out at the ocean straight in front of me. It's choppy now, frothy whitecaps slapping into each other. The insides of the waves are pressed down hard, like air is pushing them.

I look up when I hear the sound. Above me, in the air

above my island, a helicopter, its huge propeller spinning perfectly, slicing the still air into a tight neat cone of movement. It's a giant perfect insect, heavy above me, pressing the water under its invisible thumb.

I see the glint of the sun on the round, insect eye of the helicopter window. I see the competent, round little feet spin in the air below the belly. I see the gentle sway of its tail, sassy and suggestive.

I stand up and lift my hand above my head. I wave, suddenly joyful and frantic at once, hopeful and eager and ready. I think I see a waving back. Yes – a sure hand from the window. The sun glints harsh against the window of the helicopter, and hard against my eyes. I close my eyes and can imagine so clearly the dropping of the rope ladder to me, its floppy, manic twisting in the air. I imagine the gaping door of the helicopter waiting for me to rise to it. I look up, shielding my face from the sun with my hand. The sun is brilliant on the helicopter shell; no rope's been thrown to me.

I wave again, both arms now, fast and worried. This takes most of my waning strength. Then I'm practically jumping up and down, panting, waving, eager and inviting and believing. My head is hot. My eyes are wet. I close my eyes and try to catch my breath, my heaving chest.

When I open my eyes, I see it falling. A tiny colorless fleck in the wide, ungiving air. Then bigger. It's brown and square and not attached to anything. It spins down like a falling leaf towards me.

A package. It falls with a thud to the sand beside me. I see the soft poof of sand that rises like smoke when it hits. I stumble over and kneel down beside it: brown wrapping paper, bound with string and tape. I turn it right-side-up. Some of the tape has popped, the string. Some of the corners have been crushed with the fall, but I push them gently, try to smooth them out, the rumpled paper. I brush the sand off and read the address: my name.

I grab the box in both arms and hug it to my chest. I fall back into the hot hard sand. I look up to the brilliant burning sky. Is what I see the glint of sun, or the pink shape of a hand inside the window?

I know it's you, my darling. This package is from you, my dear, the final parts of me that you are sending back, the reason you have found me out again, and followed me, to hand-deliver back the final parts of me to me. It's you, my love. I see your pink hand in the shiny window.

Are you waving to me, love? Have you come to say hello or ask forgiveness?

No — it's not a wave. Just your pushing of another speck out of the gaping door. I watch it spinning in the air, a pin prick falling in an arc of sky. I see it grow, another simple block in beige, Post Office approved wrapping paper. I run, still clutching the first package in my arms, to where I think the second one will land. I hold my free arm out to it and up, as if I'll break it's fall, but I'm not fast enough, or skilled. It thumps the sand. I trip and fall and grab it in my arms. My mouth and eyes are full of sand. I see my name you've written on the label. I see the corner seam that's red and wilted, part of me inside. I squeeze the boxes in my arms and throw my head back far. I look up at the sky and up to you. I hear the humming quiet down. I see your harsh propeller pull away from me.

I drop the packages, unopened, in the sand, and leap up, flinging both my tired arms. I shout to you, bend down to snatch the packages. I jerk my head back and forth between you and the crushed boxes I'm trying to tear open. I don't know if you're coming back or when. I know what's in the packages.

I try to put them out of sight, in hidden places, dark interiors of caves, and under rocks, and off the paths I travel on my rounds to water, food and rest. But soon, I can't. Soon I'm stacking them in piles, and trying to keep them neat. There isn't room.

You come all the time and drop them always. More and more of them. I don't have time to open them, no time to wave to you. I scurry back and forth trying to stack the new ones in the ever greater piles.

They've filled up the woods. It's not a question any more of keeping them out of sight, but of hacking a path between them. They're underneath my feet, tight and hard and firm as bricks. They're high as my chest, my throat. I climb up stacks of them to put more on top.

They come so suddenly, so fast, I don't have time to make a plan. But somewhere in the back of my mind, dear love, yes, somewhere in the bottom of my heart, I tell myself, I know, that someday, darling, all of this will be yours, yes someday this will reach you, darling, all of this will add back up to you, a pile so high you'll ram back into it, your fine propeller mangling against the dense and pressing packages you have returned to me.

But I don't have time to think this. You never let me rest. I never stop. And even when I do, I don't know when I will. I just keep stacking all these boxes up. They keep arriving, constant, steady, always a surprise, day after day, each hour, every time I blink or try to breathe, just when I think I know they will, just when I think you've sent me back, just when I think there can't be anymore, when I think you'll do this to me forever, when I think, just when I think —